MUSIC STREET
NEW ORLEANS

MUSIC STREET
NEW ORLEANS

A Guide to 200
Jazz, Rock and
Rhythm & Blues Sites

Kevin J. Bozant

Po-Boy Press - New Orleans

MUSIC STREET NEW ORLEANS

No portion of this book may be reproduced in any form,
analog or digital, without written permission from
Po-Boy Press.

Text & Photographs
Copyright © 2013 Kevin J. Bozant

poboypress@yahoo.com
www.amazon.com/author/kevinjbozant

All rights reserved

ISBN-13: 978-1484944998

Books available from
Po-Boy Press – New Orleans

African American New Orleans:
A Guide to 100 Civil Rights, Culture & Jazz Sites

ISBN-13: 978-1466410589

Quaint Essential New Orleans:
A Crescent City Lexicon

ISBN-13: 978-1469951102

Crescent City Soldiers:
Military Monuments of New Orleans

ISBN-13: 978-1449913915

Music Street New Orleans:
A Guide to 200 Jazz, Rock and Rhythm & Blues Sites

ISBN-13: 978-1484944998

www.amazon.com/author/kevinjbozant

THIS BOOK IS DEDICATED TO:

Louis Moreau Gottschalk

&

James Carroll Booker III

"If you have to ask what jazz is, you'll never know."
- Louis Armstrong

INTRODUCTION

Join the "second line" with local author Kevin J. Bozant as he takes you on a neighborhood tour of over 200 music sculptures, markers, parks, murals, historic sites, statues, museums, festivals, plaques and cultural references celebrating the Jazz, Rock and Rhythm & Blues heritage of New Orleans.

At any moment in time, a musician in the Crescent City is rehearsing with the Marching 100 in the 7th Ward, playing the B-3 in Gert Town, harmonizing in Zion City, practicing piano at SUNO, jazzing it up at Preservation Hall, glorifying in a Mid-City choir, blowing a horn on Bourbon Street, marching in a Tremé brass band, second lining in a jazz funeral, conducting an orchestra for Broadway South or jamming on Frenchmen Street.

Music isn't just a way of life in New Orleans.

Music IS life in New Orleans.

In 1987, the United States Congress designated jazz "a rare and valuable national American treasure to which we should devote our attention, support and resources to make certain it is preserved, understood and promulgated." On October 31, 1994, The National Park Service (NPS) established the New Orleans Jazz National Historical Park focused on the early culture of traditional jazz. Together with the New Orleans Jazz Commission, the NPS created a series of tour maps of historic sites relating to the early history of jazz in the Crescent City. Over 60 of these sites are included here.

In 2002, The Preservation Resource Center (PRC) and the New Orleans Jazz Commission, launched the Jazz Plaque Program in an effort to identify and preserve many of the residences of local musicians associated with jazz. More than 35 of these sites are included in this book.

In New Orleans ...
Every street is Music Street.

"The Tan Canary"

JOHNNY ADAMS
Tipitina's Walk Of Fame
501 Napoleon Avenue - East Riverside

"Mr. Adams can invest life and death into every song he sings, moving from shouts to quivering phrases that seem to be dripping tears."
- **New York Times**

THE ALAMO DANCE HALL
1001 Canal Street - Central Business District

When the Junius Hart Music Store relocated, the Alamo Dance Hall moved into the second floor of this building. While the entrance was on Burgundy Street, the dancehall overlooked Canal Street. Many musicians and bands played here including banjoist and guitarist Danny Barker. NPS

THE ALAMO THEATER
1027 Canal Street - Central Business District

This small movie theater was long associated with the Fichtenburg chain. Numerous musicians played in its small pit including Indianapolis born composer and pianist J. Russel Robinson who later played in the Original Dixieland Jazz Band. The building now has a metal Art Deco façade which was added at a later date. NPS

ALGIERS POINT
Neighborhood Music Banners

Algiers was home to jazz pioneers Henry "Red" Allen, Peter Bocage, Norman Brownlee, Emmett Hardy, Manuel Manetta and "Kid" Thomas Valentine among others. Algiers has a long history of brass band music and there were a number of social halls including Perseverance Hall, the Elks' Hall and the Masons' Hall where early jazz was played. There is some jazz parading in the neighborhood today. NPS

Algiers Point is also home to the Robert E. Nims Jazz Walk of Fame presenting a series of lamp posts dedicated to influential jazz musicians.

Robert E. Nims Jazz Walk Of Fame - Algiers Point

HENRY ALLEN RESIDENCE
414 Newton Street - Algiers Point
Preservation Resource Center - 2002

Trumpet player and bandleader Henry Allen (1871-1952) and trumpet player, singer and bandleader Henry "Red" Allen Jr. (1906-1967) lived at 414 Newton Street from 1906 until 1917. Henry Allen led the Allen Brass Band, an eleven-piece group, with his brother George on snare drum and brother Samuel on tuba and alto horn. Trombonist Jack Carey was also a regular member. PRC

LOUIS "SATCHMO" ARMSTRONG

> Louis "Satchmo" Armstrong
> 1901-1971
> His trumpet and heart brought everlasting joy to the world, embodying jazz as *The Pulse of Life.*
>
> In Appreciation
> National Park Service / Tourism Cares
> April 18, 2008

From Tremé to the West Bank, there are more statues, plaques and markers celebrating the life and accomplishments of Satchmo than any other musician in the Crescent City.

This beautiful bronze statue in Armstrong Park was created by Elizabeth Catlett and paid for with donations from jazz lovers from 26 countries. It was dedicated by Lucille Armstrong in 1980.

> LOUIS ARMSTRONG STATUE
> DEDICATED BY LUCILLE ARMSTRONG
> APRIL 15, 1980
> THIS STATUE WAS PAID FOR THROUGH THE CONTRIBUTIONS OF OVER ONE THOUSAND INDIVIDUALS FROM OVER TWENTY – SIX NATIONS AROUND THE WORLD. THE STATUE PROJECT WAS COORDINATED BY THE LOUIS ARMSTRONG STATUE FUND,
> BENNY CARTER, CHAIRMAN
> FLOYD LEVIN, DIRECTOR
> ELIZABETH CATLETT, SCULPTRESS

LOUIS "SATCHMO" ARMSTRONG PLAQUES
Louis Armstrong Park
N. Rampart and St. Ann Streets - Tremé

Jazz, Rock and Rhythm & Blues

*"Every time I close my eyes blowing that trumpet of mine -
I look right in the heart of good old New Orleans ...
It has given me something to live for."*
- Louis Armstrong

**SATCHMO
N. Rampart and St. Ann Streets - Tremé
Elizabeth Catlett - 1976**

NEW ORLEANS BICENTENNIAL COMMISSION MARKER
Elk Place Neutral Ground at Cleveland Avenue - CBD

LOUIS ARMSTRONG BIRTHPLACE MARKER
Louis J. Sirgo Plaza - 715 S. Broad Street - Mid-City

Louis "Satchmo" Armstrong was born at 723 Jane Alley on August 4, 1901 in a small wood-framed house owned by his maternal Great-Grandmother, Florentine Johnson. He was the first child of Willie Armstrong and Mary Albert. The house was demolished in 1964.

COLORED WAIF'S HOME

Armstrong traditionally celebrated his birthday on July 4, 1900, a date noted by most biographers as well as on the New Orleans Bicentennial Commission marker which can be found on the neutral ground in the CBD. It was not until the mid-1980s that his true birth date of August 4, 1901, was discovered.

His music career began in his early teens when he was sent to the Colored Waif's Home at 301 City Park Avenue. He reportedly fired his stepfather's gun into the air on New Year's Eve in the 400 block of South Rampart Street. During the year he lived at the Waif's Home, he learned to read music and studied the cornet with the help of the home's musical director, Peter Davis.

>A LANDMARK OF AMERICAN MUSIC
>
>**LOUIS ARMSTRONG**
>**1900 - 1971**
>
>IT WAS AT THE COLORED WAIFS HOME FOR BOYS THAT LOUIS ARMSTRONG WAS FIRST TAUGHT TO PLAY HORN. HE WENT ON TO BECOME THE VOICE AND HEART OF AMERICAN JAZZ AND TO AFFECT THE WORLD'S TRUMPETING AND THE WORLD'S MUSIC.
>
>PRESENTED BY THE
>NATIONAL MUSIC COUNCIL,
>LOUISIANA FEDERATION OF MUSIC CLUBS,
>NATIONAL ASSOCIATION OF MUSIC MERCHANTS
>AND EXXON

MILNE BOYS HOME PLAQUE
5420 Franklin Avenue - Milneburg
This plaque disappeared after Hurricane Katrina

Eventually, the Colored Waif's Home in Mid-City merged with the Milne Boys' Home at 5420 Franklin Avenue. Armstrong never resided at the Milneburg location but visited there in 1931 along with his mentor, Peter Davis. This plaque was located to the right of the administration building entrance prior to the discovery of Armstrong's correct birth year. The plaque vanished sometime after Hurricane Katrina. Prior to its closure, the Milne Boys' Home created The Louis Armstrong Manhood Development Program to provide assistance to neighborhood boys.

LOUIS ARMSTRONG PARK

Louis Armstrong Park was carved out a central portion of the Tremé neighborhood and dedicated on April 15, 1980. The park is adjacent to Congo Square and together they form a large public space filled with jazz sculptures, bridges, gardens and fountains. The park now serves as the location for the Roots of Music Cultural Garden as well as the New Orleans Jazz National Historical Park headquarters.

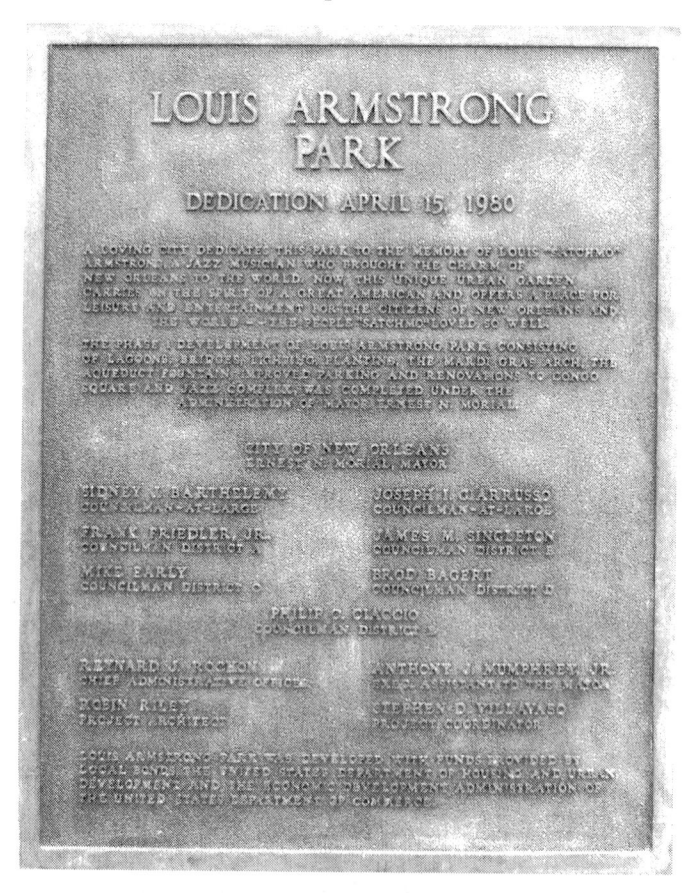

LOUIS ARMSTRONG PARK ENTRANCE
800 N. Rampart Street at St. Ann - Tremé
Dedication Plaque - April 15, 1980

A loving city dedicates this park to the memory of Louis "Satchmo" Armstrong, a jazz musician who brought the charm of New Orleans to the world. Now, this unique urban garden carries on the spirit of a great American and offers a place for leisure and entertainment for the citizens of New Orleans and the world – the people Satchmo loved so well.

LOUIS ARMSTRONG PARK ENTRANCE
800 N. Rampart Street at St. Ann - Tremé

ROBERT E. NIMS JAZZ WALK OF FAME

> # LOUIS D. ARMSTRONG
> ### August 4, 1901 - July 6, 1971
>
> ⚜ ⚜ ⚜
>
> Louis Armstrong, adoringly referred to as "Satchmo," was born August 4, 1901, but chose to celebrate his birthday on July 4th, America's Independence Day.
>
> He was the first important jazz soloist and became its most influential musician. As a trumpet virtuoso, his highly imaginative, emotionally charged playing charted a future for jazz improvisation. Revered by his fans, the King of Jazz was appropriately crowned "King Zulu" in the 1949 Mardi Gras Zulu Parade.
>
> Armstrong became an enduring figure in popular music displaying his distinctively phrased bass singing and engaging personality in a series of vocal recordings and film roles.
>
> Referred to as "The American Goodwill Ambassador," Louis Armstrong, was THE JAZZMAN of his era and truly the most renowned American musician of the 20th Century.

LOUIS ARMSTRONG PLAQUE
Robert E. Nims Jazz Walk of Fame
Bouny and Delaronde Streets - Algiers Point

LOUIS ARMSTRONG
Blaine Kern Artists - August 25, 2003
Bouny and Delaronde Streets - Algiers Point

This whimsical statue of Louis Armstrong was created and donated by Blaine Kern's Mardi Gras World. It was unveiled by The Louisiana Music Commission and the New Orleans Jazz Centennial Celebration at the dedication of the Robert E. Nims Jazz Walk of Fame in Algiers in 2003.

Robert E. Nims Jazz Walk of Fame - Algiers Point

For extra money, a young Louis Armstrong hauled coal to Storyville. There he listened to the bands playing in the brothels and dance halls of the infamous red-light district. He was especially attracted to Pete Lala's where Joe "King" Oliver performed and other famous musicians would drop in to jam.

MURAL DETAIL
Oretha Castle Haley Boulevard at Euterpe Street
Central City
Mayor's Office of Economic Development

Louis Armstrong was known by several nicknames. He had a tendency to forget people's names and simply call them Pops and the reference was eventually turned on him by his fellow musicians and biographers.

In his early days he was often referred to as Dipper, short for Dippermouth as in "Dippermouth Blues." However, the name Satchmo became the most enduring and endearing reference and was short for Satchel mouth. Armstrong, as a young boy, would dance for pennies in the streets of New Orleans. In order to protect his earnings from the other young dancers, he would scoop up the coins and store them in his cheeks. This is one of the more common explanations for this particular nickname.

LOUIS ARMSTRONG NEW ORLEANS INTERNATIONAL AIRPORT
900 Airline Drive - Kenner

In August 2001, the former Moisant Airport's name was changed to the Louis Armstrong New Orleans International Airport in honor of the famous native-born musician's 100th birthday. There is a 28 x 41 foot mural by Richard Cornelius Thomas at the south end of the central parabola lobby entitled, "Louis Armstrong and his Heavenly All-Star Band." The mural features Satchmo as the central figure surrounded by his legendary jazz colleagues. The following musicians are included in this ultimate jazz session:

Earl Turbinton, Charmaine Neville, Branford Marsalis, Pete Fountain, Ellis Marsalis, Wynton Marsalis, Harry Connick Jr., Al Hirt, Fats Domino, Sam Dinkemel, Billie Holiday, "Baby" Dodds, John Lindsey, "Jelly Roll" Morton, Mahalia Jackson, Duke Ellington, Tim Brown, Charlie Parker, Miles Davis, Edmond Hall, Dizzy Gillespie, "Buddy" Bolden, Roy "Professor Longhair" Byrd, Danny Barker, Sidney Bechet and Jack Laine.

HILTON HOTEL LOBBY AND WALK OF FAME
British Place - #2 Poydras Street - CBD

Louis Armstrong would often sign autographs with the phrase: *"Red Beans and Rice-ly Yours."*

LOUIS ARMSTRONG WAX FIGURE
Museé Conti Wax Museum Lobby
917 Conti Street - French Quarter

In 1922, Armstrong joined the exodus to Chicago, where he had been invited by his mentor, Joe "King" Oliver, to join his Creole Jazz Band. Following a storied career, the "heart and soul of American jazz" died in his sleep on July 6, 1971. He was one month away from his 70th birthday.

"THAT'S MY HOME"

*"I'm always welcomed back No matter where I roam ...
You needn't say no more 'Cause that's my home."*
- **Louis Armstrong**

"That's My Home" written by Sydney Robin
Lyrics © Universal Music Publishing Group

BASIN STREET STATION
501 Basin Street - Tremé

This visitor's information center is located at Basin Street and Orleans Avenue. The center includes several interesting exhibits relating to the history of music in New Orleans.

BACK O'TOWN

"I had a woman, livin' way Back O'Town."
- Louis Armstrong

    Immortalized by the 1930s tunes "South Rampart Street Parade" and "Back O'Town Blues" this stretch of South Rampart and Loyola Avenue from Canal Street to Howard Avenue was also known as Black Storyville. This was one of the city's most important neighborhoods relating to the development of jazz.
    The entire area, referred to as Back O'Town, represented a significant entertainment and business district defining early African American culture in New Orleans. Not much is left except the Eagle Saloon and a few vacant buildings including the remains of the Iroquois Theater and the Karnofsky business and residence.

    Back O'Town, also known at the time as the battlefield and the colored red light district, was a tough neighborhood. Louis Armstrong grew up in this area. Back O'Town included illicit gambling and prostitution houses as well as residences. The adjacent South Rampart Street corridor contained more respectable African American businesses and legitimate places of entertainment. From the turn of the century through the 1920s, Back O'Town had a concentration of saloons, social halls, dance clubs and vaudeville theaters where early jazz was played. These ranged from low-down dives, such as the Red Onion, to a middle-class ballroom like the Parisian Garden room in the Pythian Temple building. Most of the area has been redeveloped for government offices, parking areas and high-rise office buildings including the Superdome. The Red Onion, the Pythian Temple building, the Odd Fellows and Masonic Dance Halls and the Iroquois Theater are still there. Louis Armstrong's birthplace, Union Sons Hall, the Astoria Hotel and Ballroom, Spano's and several other important early structures have been demolished. NPS

BACKSTREET CULTURAL MUSEUM
1116 Henriette Delille Street - Tremé

A uniquely New Orleans institution, Backstreet is an easy walk about two blocks from the French Quarter. Exhibits include photos and regalia of jazz funerals, Mardi Gras Indians, social aid & pleasure clubs, second lines, marching brass bands and other traditions along with fascinating narration by neighborhood curators. This is as close as you can get to the essence of African American and Tremé culture in New Orleans.

> **BARBARIN FAMILY TOMB**
> (formerly L'Union Sacre Society Tomb)
>
> THE BARBARINS ARE A DYNASTY OF NEW ORLEANS JAZZ. SEVERAL GENERATIONS HAVE CARRIED THE MUSIC FROM ITS FIRST FLOWERING TO THE PRESENT DAY. INTERRED HERE IS MUSICAL PATRIARCH ISIDORE BARBARIN (1872-1960), A MAN WHO LOUIS ARMSTRONG REFERRED TO AS "POPS". ISIDORE PLAYED TRUMPET AND MELLOPHONE IN THE EXCELSIOR AND LATER THE ONWARD BRASS BAND, THE MOST FABLED BRASS BAND IN NEW ORLEANS FROM 1900 UNTIL THE END OF WORLD WAR I. HE WAS ALSO A DRIVER OF THE HORSE-DRAWN BUGGIES THAT UNDERTAKERS USED AS HEARSES UNTIL AUTOMOBILES ARRIVED. HE MARRIED JOSEPHINE ARTHIDORE AND THREE OF THEIR SONS BECAME JAZZ DRUMMERS: PAUL, LOUIS, AND LUCIEN. LUCIEN IS BURIED IN THIS TOMB, AS IS HIS SON, TRUMPET PLAYER CHARLES BARBARIN. ALSO INTERRED HERE IS ISIDORE BARBARIN'S DAUGHTER, ROSE BARBARIN BARKER COLOMBEL, MOTHER OF JAZZ LEGEND DANNY BARKER. DANNY WROTE ABOUT HIS GRANDFATHER ISIDORE IN HIS MEMOIR, "A LIFE IN JAZZ".
>
> FRIENDS OF NEW ORLEANS CEMETERIES, 2002
> WWW.FONOC.ORG

ISIDORE BARBARIN FAMILY TOMB
Musician's Tomb - St. Louis Cemetery #1
Basin and St Louis Streets - Tremé

LOUIS BARBARIN
1813 N. Robertson Street - 7th Ward

Drummer, Louis Barbarin (1902-1997) lived at 1813 N. Robertson Street in 1927. He played at Tom Anderson's Café in the Tango Belt in the 1920s and in the bands of John Robichaux, Buddy Petit, Punch Miller and George Lewis. Along with his brother, drummer Paul Barbarin and clarinetist Louis Cottrell Jr., he revived the Onward Brass Band in the 1960s. He also played at Preservation Hall until his retirement in 1982.

ADOLPH PAUL BARBARIN
1724 N. Robertson Street - 7th Ward

Drummer, composer and bandleader, Adolph Paul Barbarin (1901-1969) lived at 1724 N. Robertson Street from 1924 until 1925. He played in bands with "King" Oliver, Louis Armstrong, A. J. Piron and "Fats" Pichon. He composed "Bourbon Street Parade" and "The Second Line." Along with his brother Louis Barbarin and Louis Cottrell, he reorganized the Onward Brass Band in the 1960s and led his own band in New Orleans for over three decades. PRC

PAUL BARBARIN FAMILY TOMB
St. Louis Cemetery #2
N. Claiborne Avenue & Bienville Street - Tremé

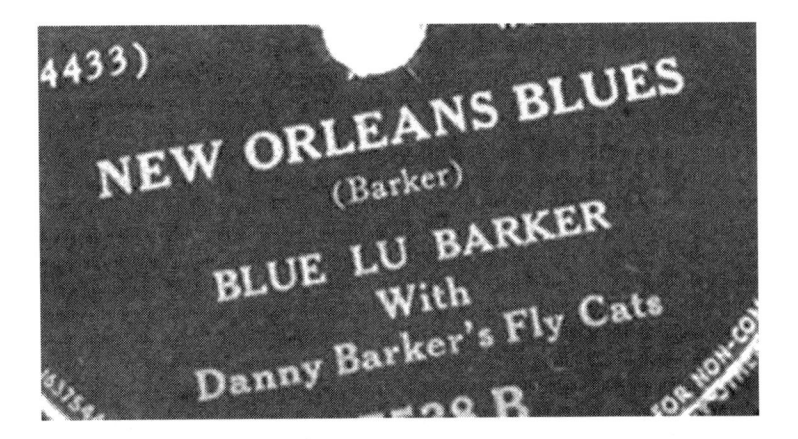

DANNY AND LOUISA "BLUE LU" BARKER

BLACK MEN OF LABOR HEADQUARTERS
Sweet Lorraine's Jazz Club
1931 St. Claude Avenue - 8th Ward

The Black Men of Labor organized in 1993 after the passing of the great jazz musician, Danny Barker. They form a second line each Labor Day out of respect for the workers of New Orleans. They carry on Barker's cultural traditions of hiring brass bands to march in parades and second lines wearing traditional black and white and playing spiritual music and mentoring young musicians from the neighborhoods.

> **BIRTHPLACE**
> **DANNY BARKER**
> **January 13, 1909**
>
> African-American Creole guitar and banjo player, songwriter, composer, singer, author, historian, teacher, storyteller, humorist, actor and painter. Jazz Hall of Fame member. Recipient of National Endowment of the Arts Music Master Award and numerous other honors. Played on more than 1,000 records of Jazz, Swing, Blues, Bebop, and Traditional. Husband of legendary singer Blue Lu Barker.

DANNY BARKER'S BIRTHPLACE
1027 Chartres Street - French Quarter

Daniel Moses Barker was a banjo player, singer, composer, ukulele player and author. He was closely related to the Barbarin family. Danny was the founder of the Fairview Baptist Church Marching Band which nurtured the early talents of Branford and Wynton Marsalis, Shannon Powell and Dr. Michael White. Danny frequently toured and recorded with his wife, "Blue Lu" Barker.

> DANNY BARKER
> JAN. 13, 1909 — MAR. 13, 1994
> GUITAR, BANJO, COMPOSER, TEACHER,
> JAZZ HISTORIAN, STORY TELLER,
> AUTHOR
> LOUISA "BLUE LU" BARKER
> NOV. 13, 1913 — MAY 7, 1998
> WIFE, SINGER, COMPOSER

DANNY & "BLUE LU" BARKER BURIAL SITE
Barbarin Family Tomb - St. Louis Cemetery #2
N. Claiborne Avenue & Bienville Street - Tremé

HILTON HOTEL WALK OF FAME
British Place - #2 Poydras Street - CBD
Paul Wegner - Sculptor

"I had certain teachers that really inspired me, like Danny Barker ... "
- Wynton Marsalis

TIPITINA'S WALK OF FAME
501 Napoleon Avenue - East Riverside

DANNY & LOUISA "BLUE LU" BARKER LAMPS
Robert E. Nims Jazz Walk of Fame - Algiers Point

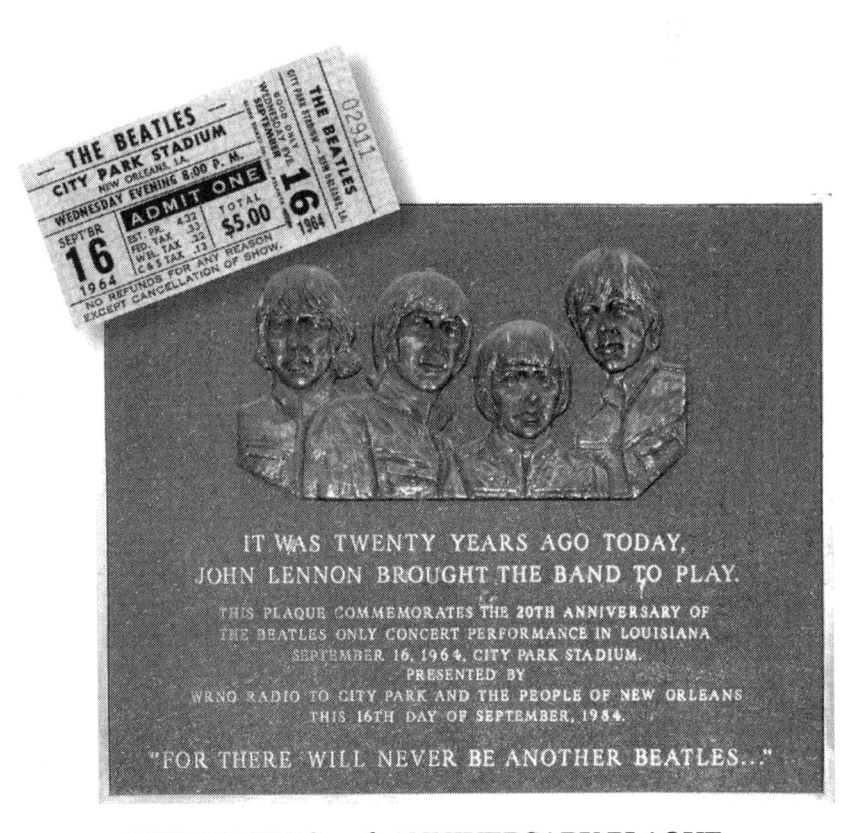

THE BEATLES 20th ANNIVERSARY PLAQUE
Tad Gormley Stadium - Marconi Drive Entrance - City Park
WRNO Radio - September 16, 1984

SIDNEY JOSEPH BECHET

THE WIZARD OF JAZZ
Louis Armstrong Park
N. Rampart and St. Ann Streets - Tremé

This copy of the original was dedicated on May 6, 1997
Abel Chrétien - 1960 - Original in Juan-Les-Pins, France

This large bronze bust celebrates the life of jazz saxophonist, clarinetist and composer, Sidney Joseph Bechet. The "Wizard of Jazz" was born in New Orleans in 1897 and died in Paris in 1958. He was one of the most important jazz soloists and saxophonists, well-known for his dynamic delivery, unique vibrato and clever improvisations.

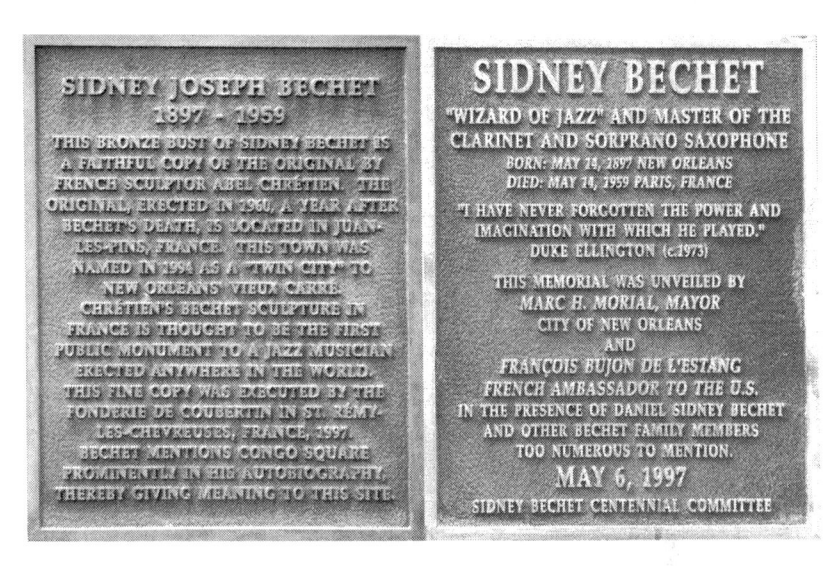

SIDNEY BECHET PLAQUES
Louis Armstrong Park
N. Rampart and St. Ann Streets - Tremé

SIDNEY BECHET CHILDHOOD HOME SITE
1716 Marais Street - New Marigny

Along with many early important jazz sites in New Orleans - such as the Half-Way House on City Park Avenue - the boyhood home of Sidney Bechet recently fell victim to the city's indiscriminate 'demolition by neglect' campaign following Hurricane Katrina. Bechet lived here from 1907 to 1914.

SIDNEY BECHET LAMP
Robert E. Nims Jazz Walk of Fame - Algiers Point

BIENVILLE HOTEL ROOF GARDEN
1040 St. Charles Avenue - Lee Circle - CBD

Built in 1920-22 by the Grunewald family and designed by Toledano, Wogan & Bernard, this hotel featured a popular roof garden. Monk Hazel's Bienville Roof Orchestra was the house band in the late 1920s. Bandleader and cornetist Hazel hired Sharkey Bonano as cornetist for the famous recordings. The roof garden is still visible. NPS

CHARLES JOSEPH "BUDDY" BOLDEN

"Simmer down; let me hear the sound of them feet."
- "Buddy" Bolden

BOLDEN NEIGHBORHOOD STREET BANNER
Oretha Castle Haley Boulevard - Central City

Central City was an English speaking, racially mixed community. Jazz greats from this neighborhood included "Buddy" Bolden, "King" Oliver, "Kid" Ory, "Papa" Celestin, Pops Foster, the Dodds and Shields brothers and Tom Zimmermann. Social halls in Central City, important in the early days of jazz, included Providence and Jackson Halls. The area has many social aid and pleasure clubs and benevolent aid societies. NPS

Robert E. Nims Jazz Walk of Fame - Algiers Point

"BUDDY" BOLDEN CHILDHOOD HOME
2309 First Street - Central City

The Bolden family lived on the right side of this shotgun double from 1887 to 1907. The house is still standing at 2309 First Street in Central City. He started out as a bandleader and became well-known for his amazing improvisations on his cornet.

This legendary cornet player is credited with being the key figure in the development of New Orleans jazz. Bolden blew his horn in dance halls and street parades all over town. He is appropriately referred to as "The First King of Jazz."

THE FIRST KING OF JAZZ
Roots of Music Cultural Garden
N. Rampart and St. Ann Streets - Tremé
Kimberly Dummons - 2010

CHARLES "BUDDY" BOLDEN
SEPTEMBER 6, 1877 - NOVEMBER 4, 1931
THIS LEGENDARY CORNET PLAYER IS OFTEN CREDITED AS THE EARLIEST JAZZ MUSICIAN AND BAND LEADER. IN DANCE HALLS AND STREET PARADES, BOLDEN WAS AMONG THE FIRST TO IMPROVISE POPULAR MUSIC USING THE BLACK BLUES AND HYMN VOCAL STYLE ON A HORN. HE IS REMEMBERED AT THE "FIRST KING OF JAZZ"
SCULPTOR: KIMBERLY DUMMONS
DEDICATED APRIL, 2010
THIS SCULPTURE WAS GENEROUSLY FUNDED BY THE EDWARD WISNER DONATION

"BUDDY" BOLDEN MARKER
Holt Cemetery - 635 City Park Avenue - Mid-City

Charles "Buddy" Bolden is buried in an unmarked grave in Holt Cemetery in Mid-City. This marker was donated by Stewart Enterprises but his exact gravesite remains a mystery.

"BUDDY" BOLDEN MARKER
Holt Cemetery - 635 City Park Avenue - Mid-City

This curious little marker is located in the rear of Holt Cemetery near a large oak tree. Ken Colyer was an English jazz musician. It is believed that Lawrence Beisly was a Bolden enthusiast who had his ashes scattered here in 1995.

Robert E. Nims Jazz Walk of Fame - Algiers Point

BOSWELL SISTERS
3937 Camp Street - Uptown

Vocalist, cellist and saxophonist, Constance Boswell (1907-1976), vocalist and pianist, Martha Boswell (1905-1958) and vocalist and violinist, Helvetia "Vet" Boswell (1911-1988) all lived at 3937 Camp Street from 1916 until they left New Orleans in 1928. They had a successful career as stars of vaudeville, radio, recordings and motion pictures. Although Martha and Vet retired from show business in 1936, Connie continued as a soloist throughout her life. PRC

NORMAN BROWNLEE
407 Delaronde Street - Algiers Point

Pianist, bandleader, instrument salesman and musicians' union official, Norman Brownlee (1896-1967) lived at 407 Delaronde Street from 1912 until 1922. He led his own Brownlee's Orchestra from 1920 to 1930, which included Emmet Hardy, Arthur "Monk" Hazel, Joseph "Sharkey" Bonano, John Wigginton Hyman and many others. His band recorded in New Orleans for the Okeh label in 1926. In 1932, he moved to Pensacola, Florida, where he became an official in the musicians' union and also continued to play piano. PRC

CANAL STREET

Canal Street is reputedly the widest main street in the United States. It gets its width and name from a proposed, but never constructed, canal that was to extend from the turning basin of the Carondelet Canal and follow a path around the Vieux Carré on a right-of-way that now includes Canal and Basin Streets. It eventually became the physical and symbolic divider between the old Creole First Municipality (Vieux Carré) and the new American Second Municipality (Faubourg Ste. Marie), now the business district. The large median was called the neutral ground, a name that is now used for medians throughout the city.

CANAL STREET BLUES
(Oliver, Armstrong)
KING OLIVER'S CREOLE JAZZ BAND

The street use went from residential to commercial in the middle nineteenth century.

During the late nineteenth and early twentieth centuries retail spaces, including music houses, dominated the street. Then small nickelodeon theaters became popular. Soon larger theaters, department stores and hotels began opening. Also included were some dance halls and radio station studios on upper floors. Some of these locations were the site of temporary or "field recording" studios for various record labels. Music permeated Canal Street then and is still around today as the street becomes a boulevard of restaurants and hotels. NPS

GEORGE J. CARRERE
4611 Chestnut Street - Uptown

Violinist, orchestra leader and music teacher, George J. Carrere (1889-1962) lived at 4611 Chestnut Street from 1917 to 1962. A graduate of Straight University, he taught at New Orleans University and gave private lessons. As a concert violinist he toured the country accompanied by pianist-composer Camille Nickerson. His brother, clarinetist-saxophonist Sidney "Goody" Carrere (1900-1953) who lived here from 1917 to 1953, played and recorded with "Papa" Celestin's Original Creole Jazz Orchestra and played with "Kid" Ory. Their nephew drummer Edwin "Beans" Bergeron (1909-1971) lived here from 1917 to 1964 and played with "Papa" Celestin, "Kid" Ory, Sidney Bechet, Louis Armstrong, Barney Bigard, "King" Oliver and marched with Fats Houston. PRC

UPTOWN BUMP
(Bolden)
KID SHOTS' NEW ORLEANS BAND

"PAPA" CELESTIN LAMP
Robert E. Nims Jazz Walk of Fame - Algiers Point

Trumpeter and bandleader "Papa" Celestin of the Original Tuxedo Jazz Band, recorded musical gems like "Marie Laveau" and "Eh, La Bas." NPS

"PAPA" CELESTIN GRAVE
Mt. Olivet Cemetery - #447
Gentilly Heights Voscoville

CHAZFEST

The Ninth Ward's answer to Jazz Fest is a ten-hour music and cultural event known as ChazFest. The festival is named after "Washboard" Chaz Leary. It takes place on the Truck Farm at St. Claude Avenue and Feliciana Street in Bywater on the Wednesday between Jazz Fest weekends. ChazFest presents an alternate view of New Orleans music, featuring local musicians.

CIVIC THEATER
533 Baronne Street - CBD

The oldest theater in New Orleans opened in 1906 as the Shubert Theater, one of a nationwide chain. Local theater architect, Sam Stone, designed it to meet specifications for legitimate theater. Through the years its name and its playbill have changed several times, offering movies and vaudeville as the Lafayette, burlesque as the Star, and legitimate theater and music as the Poche and the Civic. NPS

CLARINET MURAL

THE CLARINET

Jazz scholars refer to this neighborhood as one of the original birthplaces of jazz. The early sounds of jazz emanated from music halls in this area frequented by Buddy Bolden and other jazz greats. In honor of this historic location, Louisiana artist Robert Dafford was commissioned to paint a series of jazz murals. The clarinet has been an integral part of New Orleans style jazz bands since the music's inception in the late 1890s. This modified "Albert System" model clarinet is similar to those favored by jazz musicians who played here.

DEDICATED MAY 1, 1996

THE CLARINET HISTORICAL MARKER
330 Loyola Avenue - Back O'Town - CBD
Dedicated May 1, 1996

The African American counterpart to the Storyville District was known as Back O'Town. It was located in the current Central Business District bounded by Loyola, Canal, Baronne and Poydras but extended well beyond in all directions.

Here you will find a 16-story trompe l'oeil of a clarinet painted on the side of a hotel in honor of the various musicians who played in this neighborhood.

Vocal and Piano   4003-A
                      (2570)

BUDDY BOLDEN'S BLUES

(Morton)

JELLY ROLL MORTON

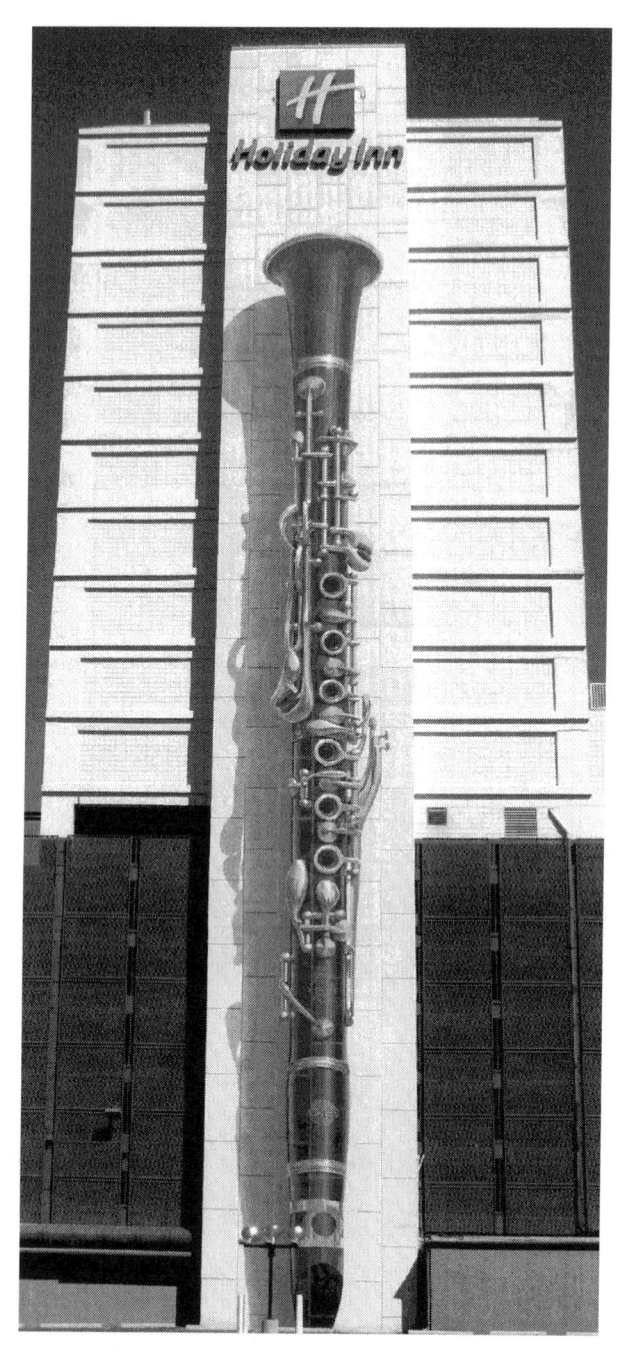

THE CLARINET MURAL
330 Loyola Avenue - Back O'Town - CBD
Robert Dafford - May 1, 1996

GEORGE "KID SHEIK" COLA(R)
939 Deslonde Street - Holy Cross

Cornetist, trumpeter, piano player and bandleader, George "Kid Sheik" Cola(r) (1908-1996) lived at 939 Deslonde Street from 1940 to 1988. He was a member of the Eureka Brass Band, the Olympia Brass Band and had his own band, The Storyville Ramblers. He recorded with those groups and with Barry Martyn's Band. He played many jobs over the years and was a regular at Preservation Hall since its inception. He toured Europe, Asia, Australia and South America. His image was featured on the 1990 Jazz and Heritage Festival poster. PRC

CONGO SQUARE

CONGO SQUARE HISTORICAL MARKER
N. Rampart and St. Ann Streets - Tremé

Congo Square, once called "Place de Negres," was one of the few areas in the South where slaves and free people of color were allowed to congregate in public prior to the Civil War. They gathered on Sundays to socialize, play music, dance and pass down their African traditions and rituals to the next generation. Hundreds of people would gather here to sing and dance. It is believed that the meeting of classically trained Creole musicians with slaves who sang a form of the blues led to the creation of that distinctly American phenomenon called jazz.

CONGO SQUARE
Roots Of Music Sculpture Garden
N. Rampart and St. Ann Streets - Tremé
Adewale Adenle - 2010

> **CONGO SQUARE**
>
> DURING THE LATE 17TH CENTURY AND WELL INTO THE 18TH CENTURIES, SLAVES GATHERED AT CONGO SQUARE ON SUNDAYS AND SANG, DANCED, AND DRUMMED IN AUTHENTIC WEST AFRICAN STYLE. THIS RICH LEGACY OF AFRICAN CELEBRATION IS THE FOUNDATION OF NEW ORLEANS' UNIQUE MUSICAL TRADITIONS, INCLUDING JAZZ.
>
> SCULPTOR: ADEWALE S. ADENLE
> DEDICATED APRIL, 2010
>
> THIS SCULPTURE WAS GENEROUSLY FUNDED BY THE EDWARD WISNER DONATION

The Commemorative Tree Grove was planted in Congo Square as a memorial to twelve jazz musicians including "Jelly Roll" Morton, "King" Oliver and Leon Roppolo. The grove is located in a quiet corner of the park near the former site of the turning basin for the old Carondelet Canal. NPS

CRESCENT CITY BLUES & BBQ FESTIVAL
Lafayette Square - Central Business District

This early October festival is sponsored by the New Orleans Jazz & Heritage Foundation. The festival is a local celebration of "Southern Soul" featuring the best in local and international R&B and blues artists. The festival is famous for its home-style barbecue.

JOSEPH JOHN DAVILLA
1930-32 Arts Street - St. Roch

Songwriter and music publisher, Joseph John Davilla (1884-1957) lived at 1930-32 Arts Street from 1920 until 1957. He composed numerous local hit songs including "The Mysterious Axman's Jazz (Don't Scare Me Papa)." He also had a national success with both "Give Me Back My Husband, You've Had Him Long E'nuff" performed on the Orpheum Vaudeville circuit by Sophie Tucker and "I Just Want Somebody, Just as Well Be You" popularized by New Orleans' own Boswell Sisters. PRC

DECATUR STREET NIGHTCLUBS

Originally the fashionable Ursuline Row, the Decatur Street nightclub area came about because of the French Market, the demise of the Gallatin Street district, the derelict nature of the lower French Quarter in the early 1900s and the closeness to the wharves. By the 1930s, the street had many bars and small dance halls with jazz bands. The clubs included Big Alcide Landry's, the Black Cat, Charlie Palooka's, Corinne's, the Filipino's, Heavey's Seventh Heaven, the Kingfish, Madame Rita's, Mama's, the Pigpen, the Popeye, Roma Café, the Rosebowl and the Wonderbar. NPS

JOHNNY DE DROIT
737 Henry Clay Avenue - Uptown

Cornetist and bandleader, John "Johnny" De Droit (1892-1988) lived at 737 Henry Clay Avenue from 1929 until 1933. He was a cornet soloist at age twelve at the Winter Garden Theater on Baronne Street and subsequently played in every New Orleans theater orchestra. During the 1920s he led his own jazz band at Kolb's Restaurant and the Grunewald Hotel Cave. He recorded for the Okeh Record Company label at sessions in New Orleans and New York. He was president of Musician's Union Local No. 174 at three different times and had a successful dance orchestra for thirty years. PRC

NEW ORLEANS BLUES
(DE DROIT)
JOHNNY DE DROIT
AND HIS NEW ORLEANS
JAZZ ORCHESTRA

DENAPOLIS TOMB
Woman holding Music and Lyre
Metairie Cemetery - Section 73 - Lakewood

Hotel De Soto, New Orleans.
(Cost $1,000,000.00)

THE DE SOTO HOTEL
(Le Pavillon Hotel)
420 Baronne Street - CBD

This hotel opened in 1906 as the Denechaud Hotel and then was known as the De Soto for many years. Louis Armstrong's mother worked here and brought home leftover food for the family. Nick LaRocca worked here as an electrician for Marks Construction Company listening to many local bands as he worked. NPS

DEW-DROP INN
2836 LaSalle Street - Central City

"MEET ME AT THE DEW DROP INN"

"Meet those fine gals, Your buddies and your pals,
Down in New Orleans on a street they call LaSalle
Down at the Dew Drop Inn,
You meet all your fine friends. Baby do drop in,
I'll meet you at the Dew Drop Inn."

"Dew Drop Inn" Penniman-Winslow
© Peyton Music BMI

THE SOUTH'S SWANKIEST NIGHT SPOT

When Frank Painia opened his little hotel on LaSalle Street in 1939, he could never have predicted it would grow into a nationally recognized entertainment venue. The Dew Drop Inn eventually hosted the likes of Ray Charles, Charles Brown, Bobby "Blue" Bland, Allen Toussaint, Shirley and Lee, Eddie "Guitar Slim" Jones, Earl King, Dave Bartholomew, Irma Thomas and James Booker. Frank Painia defied segregation laws by allowing white audiences into concerts and was often arrested for his efforts along with his customers.

DIXIE'S BAR OF MUSIC
204 St. Charles Avenue - Central Business District
701 Bourbon Street - French Quarter

From the late 1930s through the 1940s, clarinetist Dixie Fasnacht was the owner and bandleader at this legendary music spot across from the St. Charles Hotel. The club's famous wall mural by Xavier Gonzales is now on view at the Old U.S. Mint. When Dixie Fasnacht moved her establishment from the 200 block of St. Charles to Bourbon Street, she continued her policy of an all-girl jazz band with herself on clarinet. NPS

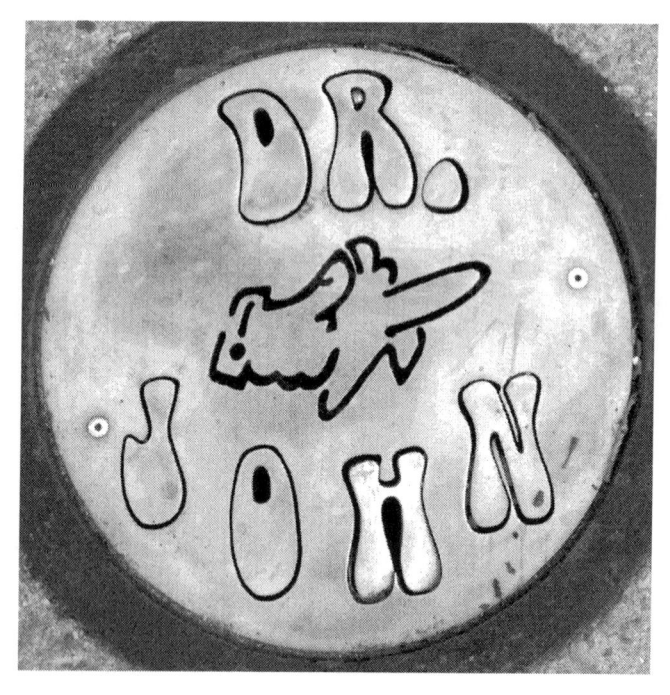

DR. JOHN
Tipitina's Banquette
501 Napoleon Avenue - East Riverside

ANTOINE "FATS" DOMINO

THE FAT MAN
New Orleans Musical Legends Park
311 Bourbon Street - French Quarter
Stephen Gibson - Sculptor

Fats Domino was born in New Orleans on February 26, 1928. He rose to national prominence with his Imperial recording of "The Fat Man" in 1949 featuring his rolling piano style. It was reportedly the first rock and roll record to sell over one million copies. Fats went on to release many hit records with his producer, Dave Bartholomew, eventually earning as many as 37 top-forty singles.

Fats Domino's house and publishing company are still located in the Lower 9th Ward.

FATS DOMINO'S HOUSE
Caffin Avenue and Marais Street - Lower 9

FATS DOMINO'S PUBLISHING COMPANY
1208 Caffin Avenue - Lower 9

Jazz, Rock and Rhythm & Blues

TIPITINA'S BANQUETTE
501 Napoleon Avenue - East Riverside

TREMÉ UNDER THE BRIDGE
N. Claiborne Avenue - Tremé
Between St. Bernard and Orleans Avenues

DREAM ROOM
426 Bourbon Street - French Quarter

Opened as the Silver Slipper by banjoist-businessman Steve Loyacano, it was later the New Slipper Club, then the Dream Room. Bandleaders Tony Parenti, Jules Bauduc, Merritt Brunies, Peter Bocage and Sharkey Bonano all played here over the years. It was also the site of trombonist Jack Teagarden's last performance. NPS

THE DREAM WORLD THEATER
632 Canal Street - CBD

Dating from around 1908, this was another Canal Street nickelodeon theater featuring New Orleans music. Composers and pianists Tom Zimmermann and Irwin Leclere were employed as house musicians. NPS

LAURENT DUBUCLET
1006 Kerlerec Street - Marigny

Jazz, Rock and Rhythm & Blues

THE DRUMMER
Besthoff Sculpture Garden - City Park
Michael Sandle - 1985

THE EAGLE SALOON
401 S. Rampart at Perdido Street - Back O'Town
Central Business District

When "Little" Jake Itzkovich closed his Eagle Loan Office in 1907, Frank Douroux opened his second tavern on the block and called it after the former loan office. The grand opening took place in January 1908 and became legendary among musicians, jazz enthusiasts and historians.

The third floor housed a ballroom used by the Odd Fellows and the Masonic Lodge. Their dances featured the likes of John Robichaux, Bunk Johnson as well as "Buddy" Bolden's Eagle Band.

During this period, "Buddy" Bolden's physical and mental health deteriorated and he was institutionalized for the rest of his life. Trombonist Frankie Dusen took over Bolden's band and renamed it the Eagle Band after the Eagle Saloon.

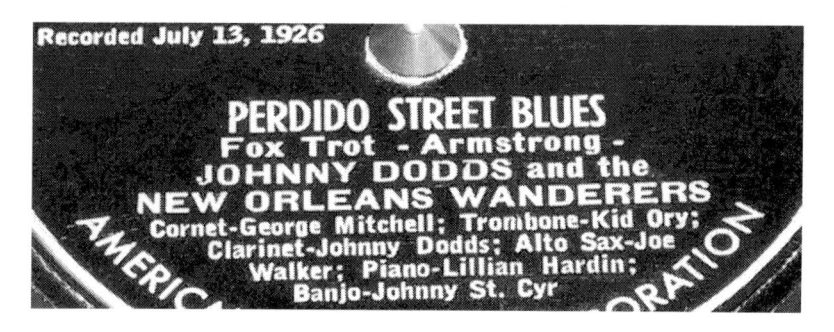

Recorded July 13, 1926
PERDIDO STREET BLUES
Fox Trot - Armstrong -
JOHNNY DODDS and the
NEW ORLEANS WANDERERS
Cornet-George Mitchell; Trombone-Kid Ory;
Clarinet-Johnny Dodds; Alto Sax-Joe Walker; Piano-Lillian Hardin;
Banjo-Johnny St. Cyr

FRANK EARLY'S "MY PLACE" SALOON
Bienville and Crozat Streets - Storyville - Tremé

Frank Early's "My Place" Saloon is one of the three remaining Storyville structures. The famous entertainer, composer and pianist, Tony Jackson, lived above the saloon where he likely composed his hit song "Pretty Baby."

THE EMPIRE THEATER
1010 Canal Street - Central Business District

This medium-sized theater, in an attractive early twentieth-century eclectic-style building, was operated by Jake Miller and his wife between 1917 and 1919. Music was provided by the Empire Jazz Band. NPS

HOMER A. EUGENE
1439 N. Claiborne Avenue - Esplanade Ridge

Guitarist, banjoist and trombonist, Homer A. Eugene (1914-1998) lived at 1439 N. Claiborne Avenue from 1946 to 1998. He played with Kid Howard's band in the 1930s, the United States Naval Band in World War II, "Kid" Thomas's band, John Handy's band, the Young Tuxedo Brass Band and recorded with Peter Bocage's Creole Serenaders on the American Music Label. PRC

ESSENCE MUSIC FESTIVAL
Morial Convention Center and the Superdome
Central Business District
July 4th weekend

The annual "Party with a Purpose" celebrates African American music and culture and presents top-notch speakers in a series of empowerment seminars. This festival attracts thousands of the most fun-loving, talented and committed people in the nation. It is one of the largest gatherings of African American musical talent in the country.

FABACHER'S RESTAURANT
137 Royal Street - French Quarter

One of two competing Fabacher restaurants, this one was run by Tony Fabacher and featured music. Bandleaders included violinist Max Fink, saxophonist Florencio Ramos and violinist-composer Anthony Maggio, who debuted his "I Got The Blues" here. NPS

FAMOUS DOOR
339 Bourbon Street - French Quarter

This Bourbon Street landmark has featured jazz for over half a century. Sharkey Bonano was a fixture for years. The Dukes of Dixieland, the Basin Street Six, Roy Liberto's Band and Santo Pecora's Band also held forth for long runs. NPS

THE FLUTE PLAYER
In Memory of Eugenie & Joseph Jones - City Park
Enrique Alférez - 1995

PETE FOUNTAIN

THE PRINCE OF MARDI GRAS
New Orleans Musical Legends Park
311 Bourbon Street - French Quarter
Stephen Gibson - Sculptor

Music Street New Orleans

HILTON HOTEL WALK OF FAME
British Place - #2 Poydras Street - CBD

HALF-FAST WALKING CLUB
Mardi Gras Fountain Detail
Lakeshore Drive - East Lakeshore

Jazz, Rock and Rhythm & Blues

Pete Fountain's Place

PETE FOUNTAIN'S PLACE
Banquette Tile Mosaic
800 Bourbon Street - French Quarter

THE FRENCH OPERA HOUSE

The INN ON BOURBON, on the corner of Toulouse and Bourbon Streets, rests on the site of the Old French Opera House, for 60 years, the cultural center of New Orleans Creole society, and the first opera house in the United States. Erected in 1859 at a cost of $118,000.00, it was opened to the public on December 1, 1859. The opera house was one of the most famous masterpieces designed by noted architect James Gallier, architect of Gallier Hall and many other classic 18th Century buildings.

FRENCH OPERA HOUSE POSTCARD
Toulouse and Bourbon Streets - French Quarter

THE FRENCH OPERA SCULPTURE
Roots of Music Cultural Garden
Louis Armstrong Park
N. Rampart and St. Ann Streets - Tremé
Steve Kline - April 2010

FRENCH OPERA

THE MAY 22, 1796 PERFORMANCE OF GRETRY'S SYLVAN IS CONSIDERED TO BE THE FIRST DOCUMENTED OPERA PRODUCTION IN NORTH AMERICA. NEW ORLEANS' RICH OPERATIC HISTORY INCLUDES AS MANY AS 400 NORTH AMERICAN PREMIERES DURING THE 19TH CENTURY. THE FRENCH OPERA HOUSE, DESIGNED BY JAMES GALLIER, OPENED IN 1859 AND BECAME THE SOCIAL AND CULTURAL CENTER OF THE CITY UNTIL IT WAS DESTROYED BY FIRE IN 1919.

SCULPTOR: STEVE KLINE
DEDICATED APRIL, 2010

THIS SCULPTURE WAS GENEROUSLY FUNDED BY THE EDWARD WISNER DONATION

**New Orleans Bicentennial Commission Marker
Elk Place Neutral Ground at Cleveland Avenue - CBD**

**FRENCH QUARTER FESTIVAL
Woldenberg Park - French Quarter - 2006**

Musicians came to the French Market to play because it was a busy place of commerce. A young Abbie Brunies played here with a trio including himself on cornet, his younger brother George on alto horn and Emmet Rogers on drums. Whether the reference is to this market or another, it has been immortalized in song by "Jelly Roll" Morton with his lyric, "I thought I heard Judge Fogarty say, thirty days in the market, take him away." Jazz is still played at the French Market today, the oldest market in the U.S.
NPS

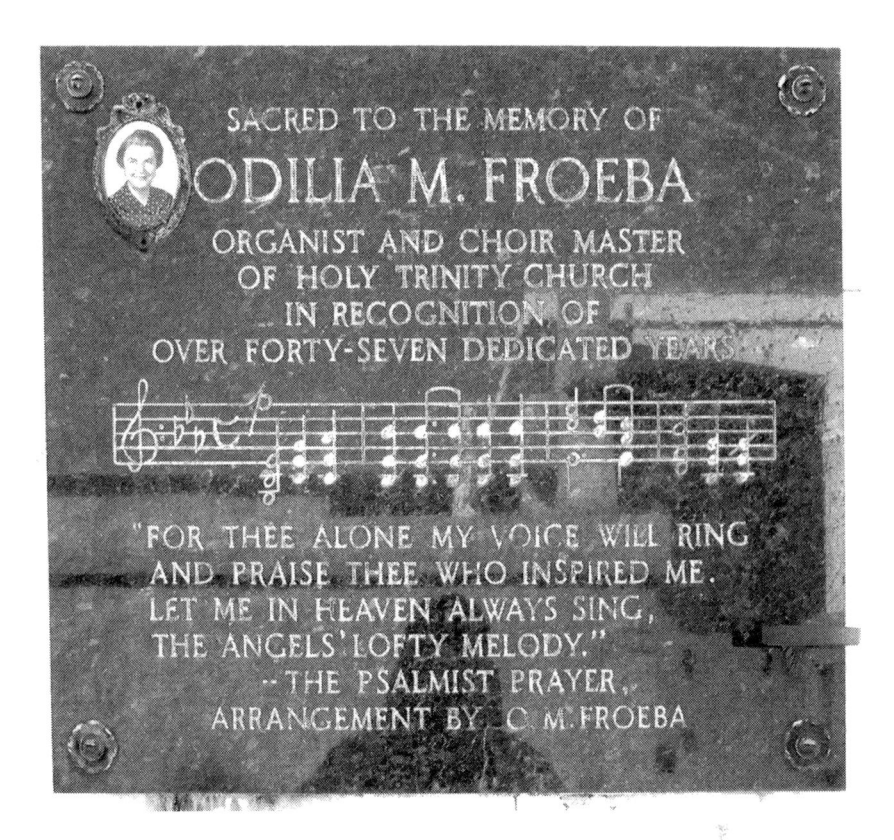

ODILIA M. FROEBA TOMB
St. Roch Cemetery - 8th Ward

It seems appropriate to include this unique music memorial to Odilia M. Froeba who provided 47 years of service as the organist and choir director of Holy Trinity Church. Holy Trinity served the Catholic German immigrants who settled in the Bywater section of New Orleans. Holy Trinity closed many years ago but the beautiful organ continues to live on at the new St. Francis Xavier Church in Metairie.

GALLATIN STREET
French Market Place - French Quarter

Named after Albert Gallatin, Secretary of the Treasury under Jefferson and Madison, these two blocks are what remains of a four-block area that extended to N. Peters Street. The others were torn down in the 1930s for the farmer's market sheds. Gallatin Street, 1840-1875, predated Storyville as one of the city's red light districts. The street is commemorated by the tune, "Gallatin Street Grind" by cornetist Johnny Wiggs. A rough area, it set the tone for the surrounding neighborhood for nearly a century. NPS

GERT TOWN

Gert Town was on the edge of the city and still being reclaimed from swamplands in the early 1900s when jazz was young. The area contained two important jazz sites - Johnson and Lincoln Parks - best known for the cutting contests around 1905 between "Buddy" Bolden's hot uptown band and John Robichaux's smooth downtown orchestra. Cutting contests were informal musical matches between bands intended to win over an audience. NPS

GRUNEWALD'S SCHOOL OF MUSIC
827 Camp Street - Central Business District

This building was the Naval Brigade Hall from 1903 until the 1940s. The Naval Brigade Band was directed by New Orleans ragtime composer, violinist and bandleader William Braun. After World War II, Grunewald Music Company opened this School of Music with black and white students under the G.I. Bill program. Instructors included Otto Finck, Willie Humphrey and Frank Federico. NPS

HACKENJOS MUSIC
930 Canal Street - Central Business District

In 1905 this was a small New Orleans publishing company for local compositions, some of which captured the essence of New Orleans music at the time. Composers Al Verges and F. C. Schmitt were associated with the company and were sheet music demonstrators in the music store. NPS

EMMETT HARDY
237 Morgan Street - Algiers Point

Cornetist and machinist, Emmet Hardy (1903-1925) lived at 237 Morgan Street in Algiers from 1920 until 1923. Emmett played with Brownlee's Orchestra, the New Orleans Rhythm Kings, in small groups with violinist Oscar Marcour, the Boswell Sisters and drummer Arthur "Monk" Hazel. During his short life he attained a legendary status as a musician and is said to have been an influence on cornetist Bix Beiderbecke as well as having an informal cutting contest with Louis Armstrong. PRC

PHIL HARRIS

HILTON HOTEL WALK OF FAME
British Place - #2 Poydras Street - CBD

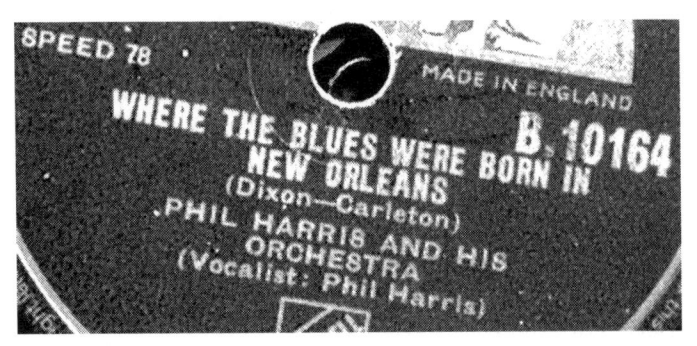

JUNIUS HART MUSIC COMPANY
1001 Canal Street - Central Business District

The music company occupied the ground floor of this building while Hart and his family lived on the upper floors. A great music merchandiser of the late nineteenth century, he published a Mexican Music series including all things "Latin" and promoted it by touring the Eighth Cavalry Mexican Band around the country. NPS

JUNIUS HART MUSIC STORE
123 Carondelet Street - Central Business District

This was Junius Hart's second location (1923-1930) and the site of the Okeh label New Orleans "field" recordings in 1924-25, featuring bands which included Johnny Bayersdorffer, Leda Bolden (with Lewis & Piron), Sterling Bose, Norman Brownlee, "Papa" Celestin, Johnny De Droit, the Halfway House Orchestra, Fate Marable, the New Orleans Rhythm Kings, Tony Parenti and John Tobin. It was also the C. G. Conn Music Company, then in 1931 became the L. Grunewald Company Music House until the late 1930s. NPS

JESSIE HILL

JESSIE HILL GRAVE
Holt Cemetery - 635 City Park Avenue - Mid-City

AL HIRT

JUMBO
New Orleans Musical Legends Park
311 Bourbon Street - French Quarter
Stephen Gibson - Sculptor

This magnificent trumpet player's music spanned the genres of jazz, classical and pop, all while recording 50 albums, receiving 21 Grammy nominations and becoming an ambassador of New Orleans jazz.

AL HIRT LAMP
Robert E. Nims Jazz Walk of Fame - Algiers Point

Al Hirt's on Bourbon Street

AL HIRT'S CLUB SITE
Bourbon Street - French Quarter

This location started as the second location for Dan's Pier 600, then became Al Hirt's Club, and then Al Hirt's Basin Street South. Hirt's group was the house band, but the club was also a venue for good jazz bands on tour. NPS

HOGAN JAZZ ARCHIVE
Jones Hall - Tulane University
7001 Freret Street - Uptown

The Hogan Jazz Archive is part of the Special Collections Division of Tulane's Howard Tilton Memorial Library. The collection includes a treasure trove of jazz recordings, videos, books, oral histories, personal memorabilia, discographies, sheet music and photographs of jazz musicians.

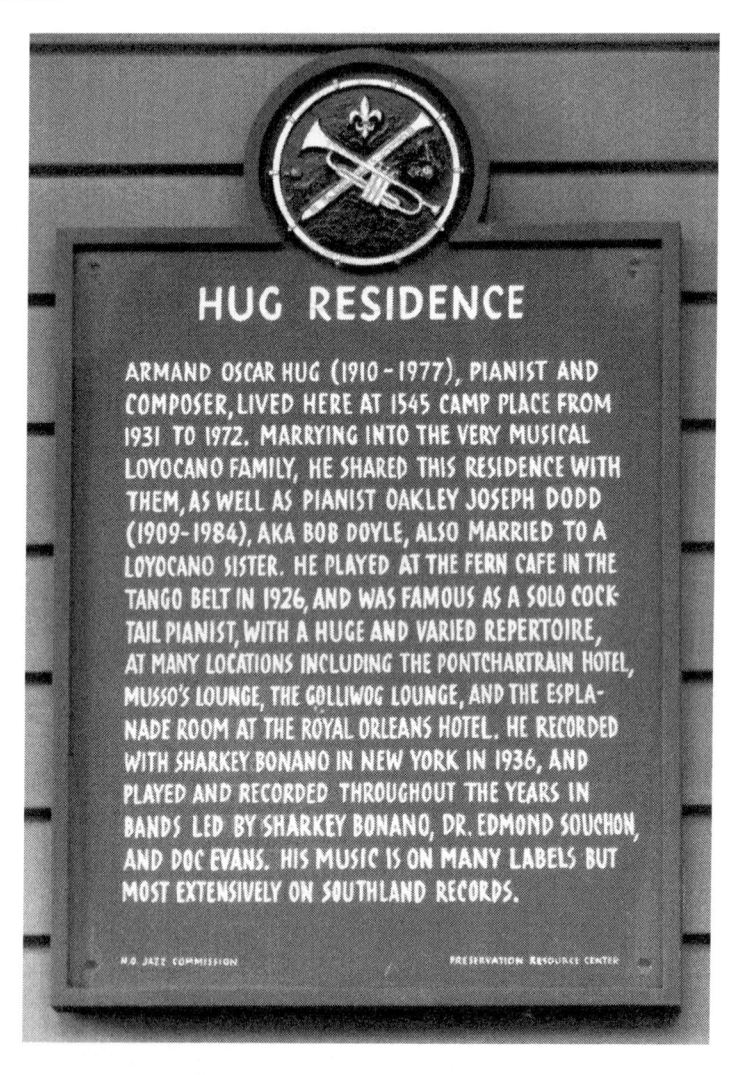

ARMAND HUG
1545 Camp Place - Coliseum Square

HUMPHREY FAMILY LAMP
Robert E. Nims Jazz Walk of Fame - Algiers Point

WILLIE J. HUMPHREY
2315 Cadiz Street - Uptown

Jazz clarinetist, Willie J. Humphrey (1900-1994) lived for a time at 2315 Cadiz Street in Uptown New Orleans. He was born into a very musical family. His father, Willie E. Humphrey, was a clarinetist and music teacher. His brothers Percy and Earl were also very successful musicians. Willie played with "King" Oliver, the Excelsior Brass Band, Paul Barbarin and Sweet Emma. In his later years he was a prominent member of the Preservation Hall Jazz Band.

IRISH CHANNEL

The Irish Channel was mostly a white working-class community during the early days of jazz. Musicians from the channel included Tom Brown, the five Brunies brothers, Nick LaRocca, and Tony Sbarbaro. Social halls here included the Cherry Pickers Hall (extant), the Corner Club and the Jesters Club. Much of the residential area looks as it did during the jazz age. NPS

IROQUOIS THEATER
413 South Rampart Street - Back O'Town - CBD

The Iroquois Theater was constructed in late 1911 and featured vaudeville and other musical programs until 1920. Many prominent musicians of the day performed here including James "Steady Roll" Johnson, Clarence Williams, guitarist Lonnie Johnson, singer Edna Landry, Lizzie Miles and of course, Louis Armstrong.

Armstrong wrote in his memoirs that he went to see movies at the Iroquois for ten cents. He claims to have once covered his face with flour and won an amateur contest there. The Iroquois was a cornerstone of black entertainment in New Orleans.

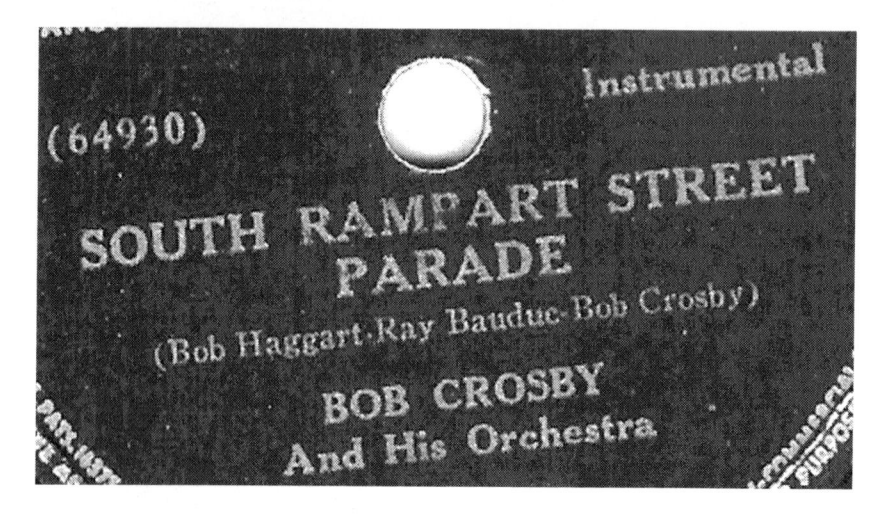

ITALIAN HALL
2010 Esplanade - French Quarter

This imposing complex was assembled out of old buildings (one by architect James Gallier, dating to 1835) and new construction from between 1912 and 1920. As the Unione Italiana, which combined many Italian benevolent societies, it was the home of both the Contessa Entellina Society Band, made up of Albanian-Sicilian Italian-Americans and the Roma Band of Sicilian Italian-Americans. During their rivalry, a musician could be in one, not both. Many jazz bands played here for dances including the New Orleans Rhythm Kings upon their return to New Orleans. In 1929, it housed the Jones-Collins Astoria Hot Eight recording session, the first racially-integrated recording in New Orleans. Westwego-born clarinetist Sidney Arodin (Arnondin) jumped the color barrier. PRC

J & M RECORDING STUDIO ENTRANCE
Rampart and Dumaine Streets - French Quarter

FIRST RECORDING STUDIO OF
COSIMO MATASSA
BUILT CIRCA 1835
WITH GALLERIES LIKELY ADDED IN THE 1850S.

IN 1944, J&M AMUSEMENTS ACQUIRED THE BUILDING, AND COSIMO MATASSA SOON OPENED J&M RECORDING STUDIO.

OSCAR "PAPA" CELESTIN, DANNY BARKER, AND THE DUKES OF DIXIELAND RECORDED JAZZ HERE.

THE "NEW ORLEANS SOUND" DEVELOPED FROM PIONEERING RHYTHM & BLUES AND ROCK & ROLL RECORDINGS MADE HERE BETWEEN 1947 AND 1956 BY PAUL GAYTEN, ANNIE LAURIE, ROY BROWN, DAVE BARTHOLOMEW, FATS DOMINO, PROFESSOR LONGHAIR, SMILEY LEWIS, JOE TURNER, GUITAR SLIM, SHIRLEY & LEE, LLOYD PRICE, JERRY LEE LEWIS, LITTLE RICHARD, RAY CHARLES, AND OTHERS.

J & M RECORDING STUDIO

From 1947-1956, J&M Studios, owned and operated by Cosimo Matassa, produced the records that helped give birth to rock and roll. Along with producer and arranger Dave Bartholomew, Matassa recorded sessions by pioneers Fats Domino, Little Richard, Bartholomew, Professor Longhair, Smiley Lewis, Lloyd Price, Roy Brown, and Shirley and Lee, among many others.

This building housed the legendary J & M Studio of Cosimo Matassa who created the "New Orleans Sound" with local musicians such as Professor Longhair, Dave Bartholomew, Fats Domino, Guitar Slim, Shirley & Lee, Lloyd Price, Ernie K-Doe, Danny Barker and Clarence "Frogman" Henry. National artists included Little Richard, Ray Charles and Jerry Lee Lewis. Cosimo also recorded may other jazz greats such as "Papa" Celestin, Raymond Burke and the original Dukes of Dixieland.

MAHALIA JACKSON

New Orleans Bicentennial Commission Marker
Elk Place Neutral Ground at Cleveland Avenue - CBD

MAHALIA JACKSON
OCTOBER 26, 1911 - JANUARY 27, 1972
MAHALIA JACKSON WAS BORN IN NEW ORLEANS AND BECAME KNOWN AS "THE WORLD'S GREATEST GOSPEL SINGER." THROUGH CONCERTS AND RECORDINGS, HER POWERFUL VOICE INTRODUCED BLACK GOSPEL MUSIC TO AN INTERNATIONAL PUBLIC. SHE SANG IN SUPPORT OF DR. MARTIN LUTHER KING, JR. AND THE CIVIL RIGHTS MOVEMENT.
SCULPTOR: ELIZABETH CATLETT
DEDICATED APRIL, 2010
THIS SCULPTURE WAS GENEROUSLY FUNDED BY THE EDWARD WISNER DONATION

THE WORLD'S GREATEST GOSPEL SINGER
Louis Armstrong Park
N. Rampart and St. Ann Streets - Tremé
Elizabeth Catlett - 2010

The inscription on Mahalia's tomb in Providence Memorial Park in Kenner lists her birthdate as 1912. She was actually born on October 26, 1911 on Pitt Street in the Black Pearl neighborhood of New Orleans. Her family worshipped at Mt. Moriah Baptist Church on Millaudon Street. At the age of four, she began singing in the choir until the eighth grade. She then moved to Chicago. Her musical upbringing in New Orleans exposed her to traditional church music, gospel and jazz and her illustrious career speaks for itself.

MOUNT MORIAH MISSIONARY BAPTIST CHURCH
147 Millaudon Street - Black Pearl

Tipitina's Banquette Plaque

JAZZ FUNERAL

"Music here is as much a part of death as it is of life."
- Sidney Bechet

    This honorary funeral procession through the streets of New Orleans is generally reserved for deceased musicians, Indian Chiefs and other prominent residents of New Orleans. A grand marshal leads fellow musicians and mourners with a dirge. Following the burial, the music becomes more joyful and spirited. A second line follows with umbrellas and waving handkerchiefs. The Yoruba, according to John Scott, believed that if they bury you in the rain it is a sign that you lived a good life. This may explain the tradition of dancing and parading with umbrellas.

    There is a saying that when someone dies in New Orleans you book a brass band - then you call the coroner!

JAZZ & HERITAGE FESTIVAL BANNERS
North Rampart Street - Tremé

JAZZ & HERITAGE FESTIVAL
Fair Grounds Race Course
1751 Gentilly Boulevard - Mid-City
Last weekend in April and the first weekend in May

Mahalia Jackson returned home in 1970 to appear at the first New Orleans Jazz & Heritage Festival held in Congo Square. Today the whole world seems to converge at the Fair Grounds every year due to the festival's growing popular appeal and cultural significance.

The festival features multiple stages of music with evening concerts and workshops held at venues around town. Locally and nationally known musicians provide a wide variety of styles including jazz, pop, gospel, rock and R&B; surrounded by a generous offering of local crafts and internationally celebrated cuisine. You will also encounter brass bands, second lines and occasional appearances by the Mardi Gras Indians.

The New Orleans Jazz & Heritage Foundation, Inc., whose mission is "to promote, preserve, perpetuate and encourage the music, art, culture and heritage indigenous to the New Orleans area," sponsors the Jazz Fest.

JAZZ & HERITAGE CENTER
1225 N. Rampart Street - Tremé

The Jazz and Heritage Center offers classroom space, dance and music rehearsal studios as well as facilities for concerts and lectures.

JAZZ IN THE PARK
Louis Armstrong Park - Tremé
People United for Armstrong Park

Jazz in the Park is a free concert series held every Thursday afternoon during September and October. In addition to music, events include second lines, Congo Square Arts and Crafts Village and assorted local food and drink.

JAZZ MUSEUM - UNITED STATES MINT
400 Esplanade Avenue - French Quarter

The Louisiana State Museum's collection traces the history of jazz in New Orleans from its simple roots to its international recognition as a unique American art form. Visitors will find an amazing collection of memorabilia, sheet music and instruments once belonging to many of our local jazz greats. Some of the artifacts of New Orleans jazz include two of Louis Armstrong's horns, Jack Laine's bass drum, Sidney Bechet's saxophone, Bix Beiderbecke's cornet and Irving Fazola's clarinet.

JAZZ NATIONAL HISTORICAL PARK
Louis Armstrong Park
St. Philip Street at Henriette Delille - Tremé

THE JAZZ PLAYER
Harrah's Casino Lobby - Central Business District
Designed by H. Conversano Designs
Chiodo Entertainment

HISTORIC ALGIERS

Algiers, established in 1719, is the second oldest neighborhood in New Orleans. Originally called the "King's Plantation," it was first used as the location for the city's powder magazine, a holding area for the newly arrived African slaves, and the first port of call for the displaced Cajuns.

Developed as a town by Barthelemy Duverje, Algiers expanded due mainly to the shipbuilding and repair industries of the dry docks and the extensive railroad yards. A large part of the town in the area surrounding the Courthouse was destroyed by fire in 1895 but rose again like a Phoenix from the ashes.

Many Jazz and Blues "greats" have called Algiers home including Lester Young, Memphis Minnie, Henry "Red" Allen, George Lewis, and "Kid" Thomas Valentine.

The charm and architecture of old Algiers is New Orleans' "hidden jewel."

Kevin Herridge
President, 2002
Algiers Historical Society

Vinnie Pervel
President, 2002
Algiers Point Association

ROBERT E. NIMS JAZZ WALK OF FAME
Henry "Red" Allen Ferry Landing - Algiers

Located just a Mississippi River ferry ride from downtown New Orleans, the Robert E. Nims Jazz Walk of Fame presents a series of lamp posts dedicated to influential jazz musicians. The walk begins near the base of the statue of Louis Armstrong that was created by Blaine Kern Artists. A brochure is available at nps.gov/jazz or one can take a self-guided audio tour atop the levee while witnessing great views of downtown New Orleans.

JUNG HOTEL, NEW ORLEANS, LA.   105724

THE JUNG HOTEL
1500 Canal Street - Central Business District

This hotel was listed on the National Register of Historic Places in 1982. The Tulane Room was the site of jazz dances and the Jung Hotel Roof Garden featured the hot music of the Ellis Stratakos Orchestra in the late 1920s and early 1930s. NPS

KARNOFSKY FAMILY BUSINESS AND RESIDENCE
427 South Rampart Street - Back O'Town/CBD

The Karnofsky family played a significant role in the early life of Louis Armstrong. He worked on their junk wagons and regularly ate meals with the family. He also delivered coal for the Karnofskys, sometimes to the brothels of Storyville. Louis remembers blowing a small tin horn while riding the family's delivery wagon around town. The Karnofsky family eventually lent him the money to buy a real horn from a pawn shop.

Morris Music, one of the city's earliest jazz record stores, was started at this location. It was operated by Morris Karnofsky, a boyhood friend of Armstrong's.

ERNIE K-DOE'S MOTHER-IN-LAW LOUNGE
1500 N. Claiborne Avenue - Tremé
Murals by Daniel Fuselier

The Mother-in-Law Lounge is a local shrine to the music and memory of the self-proclaimed "Emperor of the World," Ernie K-Doe.

In 1994, Ernie's wife, Antoinette K-Doe, opened the lounge to try to revitalize the R&B hit maker's career. In doing so, they both became local icons as well as endearing New Orleans characters.

K-Doe passed away July 5th, 2001, but Antoinette kept the lounge going with a life-size mannequin of "Ernie" who kept watch over the bar and made occasional public appearances.

As of 2013, the lounge has been reopened by Kermit Ruffins and is called Kermit's Tremé Mother-In-Law Lounge.

"And don't come back no more, Mother-in-Law!" - **Ernie K-Doe**

"I'm Cocky, But I'm Good." - **Ernie K-Doe**

K-DOE TOMB
St. Louis Cemetery #2 - Tremé
All Saints' Day - 2006

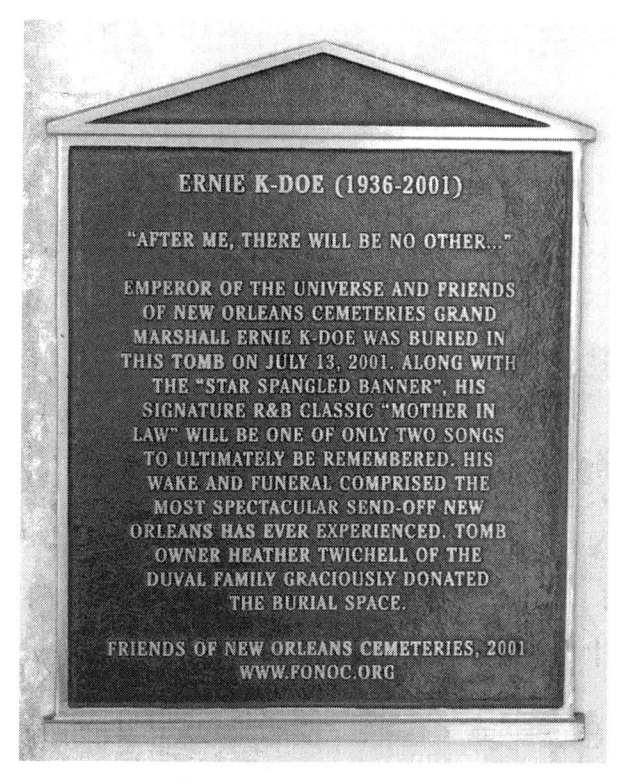

> **ERNIE K-DOE (1936-2001)**
>
> "AFTER ME, THERE WILL BE NO OTHER..."
>
> EMPEROR OF THE UNIVERSE AND FRIENDS OF NEW ORLEANS CEMETERIES GRAND MARSHALL ERNIE K-DOE WAS BURIED IN THIS TOMB ON JULY 13, 2001. ALONG WITH THE "STAR SPANGLED BANNER", HIS SIGNATURE R&B CLASSIC "MOTHER IN LAW" WILL BE ONE OF ONLY TWO SONGS TO ULTIMATELY BE REMEMBERED. HIS WAKE AND FUNERAL COMPRISED THE MOST SPECTACULAR SEND-OFF NEW ORLEANS HAS EVER EXPERIENCED. TOMB OWNER HEATHER TWICHELL OF THE DUVAL FAMILY GRACIOUSLY DONATED THE BURIAL SPACE.
>
> FRIENDS OF NEW ORLEANS CEMETERIES, 2001
> WWW.FONOC.ORG

ERNIE K-DOE PLAQUE
K-Doe Tomb - St. Louis Cemetery #2 - Tremé

Less than a year after Ernie passed, his real-life mother-in-law, Leola Wallace Clark, died and was buried with him in the same tomb.

> **ANTOINETTE K-DOE**
> (February 3, 1943 - February 24, 2009)
>
> Spouse of Ernie K-Doe, who added years to his life, and owner of the Mother in Law Lounge, a gathering place dedicated to perpetuating classic New Orleans R. & B. Antoinette breathed new life into Carnival traditions, especially the Baby Dolls, and All Saints' Day observances. She was a magnificent chef and clothing designer and did much to revive New Orleans following Hurricane Katrina.
>
> Friends of New Orleans Cemeteries

ANTOINETTE K-DOE PLAQUE

Antoinette, who helped revitalize the Mardi Gras Baby Dolls tradition, died on Mardi Gras morning in 2009. She is buried alongside Ernie in St. Louis Cemetery #2.

FREDDIE KEPPARD LAMP
Robert E. Nims Jazz Walk of Fame - Algiers Point

THE KING'S ROOM
811 Iberville Street - French Quarter

Because of its location as part of the Iberville Street strip, this small night club under its various names was probably one of the few that survived the entertainment transition from the Tango Belt to Bourbon Street. It featured pianist Armand Hug in the early 1960s. NPS

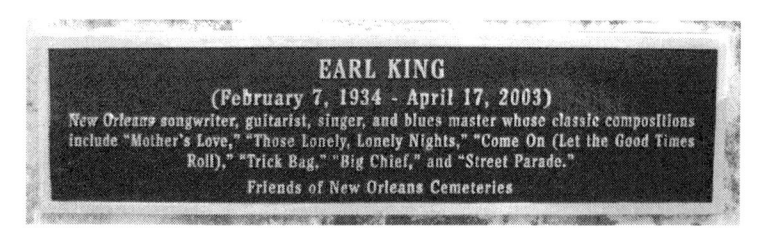

EARL KING PLAQUE
K-Doe Tomb - St. Louis Cemetery #2 - Tremé

THE KING FISH BEER PARLOR
1101 Decatur Street - French Quarter

The King Fish, probably known briefly as the Pig Pen, was another of the more long-lived clubs. Operated by Vincent Serio Jr. and Arthur Schott, aka the King Fish, the musicians featured included George Lewis, Billie Pierce, Dee Dee Pierce, Burke Stevenson and Smilin' Joe (Pleasant Joseph). NPS

KOLB'S
KOLB'S GERMAN RESTAURANT
125 St. Charles Avenue - CBD

This famous German Restaurant was founded in 1898 by Conrad Kolb. Cornetist and bandleader, Johnny De Droit led his band here in the 1920s. The Kirst Brothers played dinner music, German bands celebrated Oktoberfest and many other musicians played for dances and parties. NPS

RONNIE KOLE
New Orleans Musical Legends Park
311 Bourbon Street - French Quarter

EMILE "STALEBREAD" LACOUME
2723 Iberville - Mid-City

Emile "Stalebread" Lacoume was a zither player, guitarist, pianist and banjoist who lived at 2723 Iberville Street in Mid-City. He was an original member of the legendary Razzy Dazzy Spasm Band. This small group of street urchins performed on the banquettes of Storyville in the 1890s. Some jazz historians regard them as the earliest jazz band.

LAFAYETTE SQUARE
Gallier Hall - Central Business District

First known as Place Gravier, it became Lafayette Square after Lafayette's visit to New Orleans in 1825. In 1864, famed bandleader Patrick S. Gilmore presented his legendary concert with a 500-member band, a choir of thousands of school children and a bell ringer. It has been the site of performances for inaugurations, yearly pilgrimages by school bands and endless jazz concerts for over 150 years. Originally the headquarters for the 2nd Municipality, Gallier hall was constructed in 1845 and designed by James Gallier Sr., renowned New Orleans architect. It became City Hall for a century. For a half-century it has been a reception hall, and throughout it all, the site of constant music and theater. NPS

Robert E. Nims Jazz Walk of Fame - Algiers Point

GEORGE V. "PAPA" JACK LAINE
538 St. Ferdinand Street - Marigny

    Bandleader, drummer, alto horn player, string bassist, blacksmith and prize fighter, George V. "Papa" Jack Laine (1873-1966) lived at 2424 Chartres Street in 1904 and 538 St. Ferdinand Street in 1917. He was a successful bandleader for over three decades and the members of his Reliance Brass Bands became some of the most famous jazz musicians in history. Many of his musicians were also members of Tom Brown's Band from Dixie, The Original Dixieland Jazz Band, The Louisiana Five, Jimmy Durante's Original New Orleans Jazz Band, The New Orleans Rhythm Kings, The Halfway House Orchestra, Tony Parenti's Liberty Syncopaters and Johnny De Droit and his New Orleans Jazz Orchestra. PRC

LALA'S BIG "25"
Main Entrance Reproduction
Basin Street Station - 501 Basin Street - Tremé

LA LOUISIANE RESTAURANT
725 Iberville Street

Operated in its earlier days by the Alciatore Family and later by "Diamond Jim" Moran, this fancy French restaurant featured many bands over the years, including those of John Robichaux and Herbie Pelligrini.
NPS

DOMINIC "NICK" LaROCCA
Robert E. Nims Jazz Walk of Fame - Algiers Point

Cornetist and bandleader, Dominic "Nick" LaRocca (1889-1961) lived at 928 Jackson Avenue from 1928-1942 and at 2216-18 Constance Street from 1942-1961. He initially played in neighborhood bands, then with William Braun's Brass Band and Jack Laine's Reliance Bands. He left New Orleans in 1916, as a cornetist with Johnny Stein's Band in order to pursue a job offer in Chicago. After the departure of Stein, LaRocca eventually led the Original Dixieland Jazz Band. In 1917, the ODJB made the first jazz recording for Victor Records in New York. After an astounding recording career in the U.S. and England, the band broke up in the middle 1920s but briefly reorganized and made more recordings in 1936. After returning to New Orleans for the second time, LaRocca worked as a building contractor, led a small band for occasional jobs, played the banjo and composed several pieces of music. PRC

GEORGE LEWIS RESIDENCE
827 St. Philip Street - French Quarter

Clarinetist, George Lewis (1900-1968) lived at 827 St. Philip Street. This was the location where the 1943 recording of Lewis's "Burgundy Street Blues" took place. It was also the site of the recording session for Bunk Johnson's Brass Band in 1945. NPS

George Lewis
and his New Orleans Music

GTJ 16
MM498 (LK168)

New Orleans
5.6.50

BURGUNDY ST. BLUES
(Lewis)

George Lewis (cl) Alton Purnell (p)
Lawrence Marrero (bjo) Alcide Pavageau (b)

LINCOLN BEACH
14000 Hayne Boulevard - Little Woods
New Orleans East

In 1939, a section of beach on Lake Pontchartrain in Little Woods was set aside as a swimming area for African Americans. By the early 1950s, Lincoln Beach had become a vacation destination with amusement park rides and musical acts such as Fats Domino, the Ink Spots, Ray Charles and Nat King Cole. Lincoln Beach was a prominent fixture in the lives of the New Orleans African American community until 1964 when Pontchartrain Beach Amusement Park was integrated.

This sign is a rusty memory of the parking lot, but the actual site on the lake is still used for fishing and swimming.

THE LITTLE GEM SALOON
Renovated - 2013
South Rampart at Poydras Street - Back O'Town - CBD

This building originally housed Frank Douroux's Little Gem Saloon (1904-09), David Pailet's Loan Office (1926-49) and then Pete's Blue Heaven Lounge (1950s). This prominent corner housed three landmark businesses associated with jazz and was often both a starting and ending place for Zulu Social Aid and Pleasure Club funerals. NPS

LOEW'S STATE THEATER
1108 Canal Street - Central Business District

Now the State Palace, this theater opened in 1925 and was designed by Thomas W. Lamb, the world's most prolific theater architect. The orchestra featured clarinetist Charlie Scaglioni and trumpeters Leo and Lucian Broekhoven. NPS

THE LUTE PLAYER
LL&E Building - 909 Poydras Street - CBD
Enrique Alférez - Bronze - 1988

MARDI GRAS LOUNGE
333 Bourbon Street - French Quarter

This club, known as Sid Davilla's Mardi Gras Lounge, featured Lizzie Miles as well as Freddie Kohlman's band and others. Owner and clarinetist Sid Davilla usually sat in with the band on the last set. NPS

MARTIN'S SALOON
621 Iberville Street - French Quarter

This bar, operated by Albert J. and Emile Martin, was strategically located at the corner of Exchange Alley and was a hangout for musicians waiting for calls for jobs. Jack Laine and others recruited from those in the bar and in the street. The interior and exterior of this building are little changed from their days as Martin's. NPS

MANUEL JOHN MELLO
1025 Bartholomew Street - Bywater

Cornetist and bandleader, Manuel John Mello (1888-1961) lived at 1025 Bartholomew Street from 1917 until 1961. He played with Weinmunson's Band, Johnny Fischer's Band, Fischer's Military Band and was the leader of one of Jack Laine's Reliance Brass Band units. He later led his own Mello's Original Jazz Band. He worked most of his life as a sugar maker and spent a great deal of his time in Oriente Providence in Cuba. PRC

LIZZIE MILES
1508 Pauger Street - Marigny

Singer, Elizabeth Mary Landreaux, aka Lizzie Miles (1895-1963) lived at 1508 Pauger Street (formerly Bourbon Street) in 1896. Her specialty was singing in both English and in a New Orleans Creole French patois. She sang in churches, with "King" Oliver, "Kid" Ory and Bunk Johnson before traveling with circus shows. She later recorded with "Jelly Roll" Morton and Clarence Williams. During the 1940s through the 1960s she sang or recorded with a diverse groups of musicians including Frank Federico, Paul Barbarin, Sharkey Bonano, George Lewis, Tony Almerico, Freddie Kohlman, Red Camp and Bob Scobey. PRC

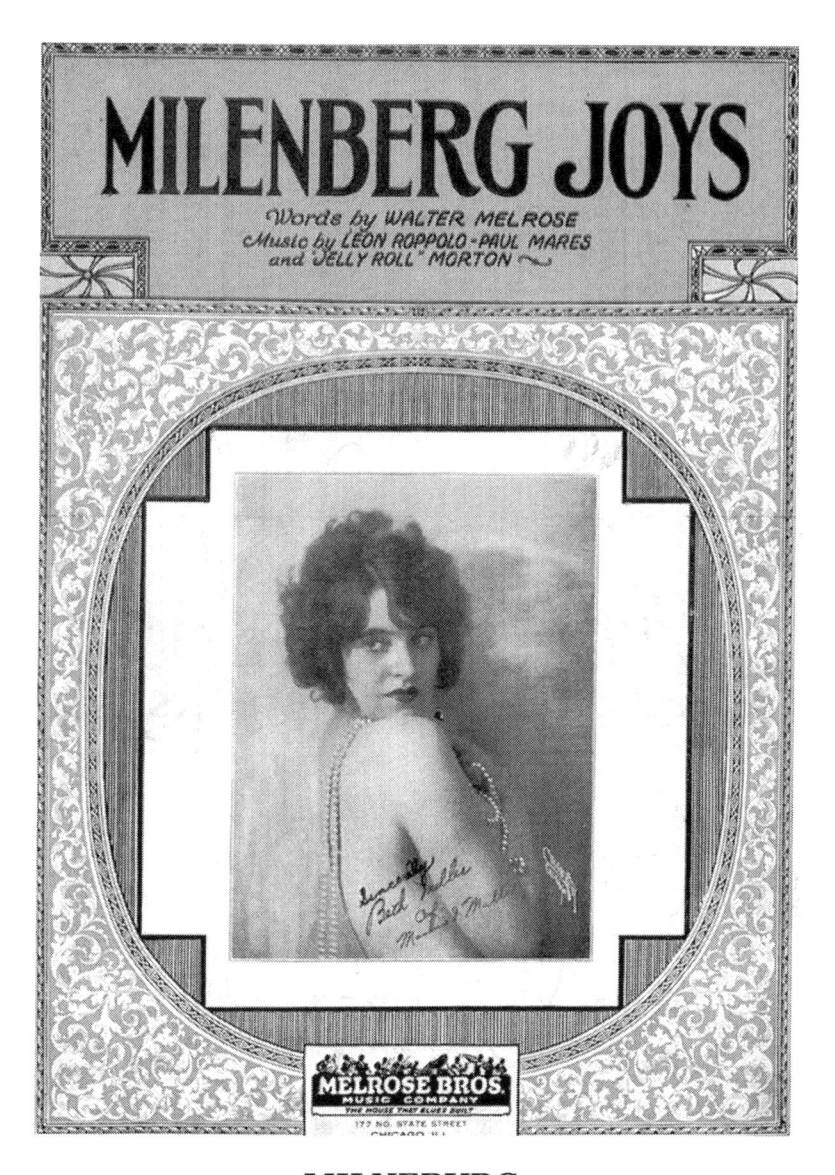

MILNEBURG

The area along the lakefront at the end of Elysian Fields was called Milneburg for former resident and businessman, Alexander Milne. Once called Old Lake End, it was a resort area important in the early history of jazz. Milneburg eventually became the site of the Pontchartrain Beach Amusement Park. It was historically mispronounced (MIL en berg) resulting in a famous jazz tune titled, "Milenburg Joys."

ALLISON MONTANA
"Chief Of Chiefs"

BIG CHIEF "TOOTIE" MONTANA
Yellow Pocahontas "Chief of Chiefs"
Roots of Music Cultural Garden
N. Rampart and St. Ann Streets - Tremé
Sheleen Jones-Adenle - 2010

ALLISON "BIG CHIEF TOOTIE" MONTANA
DECEMBER 16, 1922 - JUNE 27, 2005

YELLOW POCAHONTAS MARDI GRAS INDIAN TRIBE / "CHIEF OF CHIEFS" A NEW ORLEANS CULTURAL ICON AND INTERNATIONALLY RECOGNIZED MASTER CRAFTSMAN IN THE BUILDING TRADE, BIG CHIEF MONTANA MASKED AS A MARDI GRAS INDIAN FOR OVER 50 YEARS. HE DIED IN CITY COUNCIL CHAMBERS DEFENDING THE MARDI GRAS INDIAN TRADITION.

SCULPTOR: SHELEEN JONES-ADENLE
DEDICATED APRIL, 2010

THIS SCULPTURE WAS GENEROUSLY FUNDED BY THE EDWARD WISNER DONATION

MONTELEONE HOTEL
214 Royal Street - French Quarter

The Monteleone was designed in 1908 by architects Toledano & Wogan. Featured artists included a young Liberace, Louis Prima and the Dukes of Dixieland on the roof. The Monteleone boasts almost a century of music events and headliners. NPS

MORRIS MUSIC
164 S. Rampart Street - CBD

Morris Music's last and longest location was in this fine building at 164 S. Rampart Street at Common. It was a meeting place for musicians. Louis Armstrong visited his boyhood friend Morris Karnofsky and all of his musician buddies here on his many return trips to the city. NPS

"JELLY ROLL" MORTON

MISTER "JELLY ROLL"
Museé Conti Wax Museum - Jazz Exhibit
917 Conti Street - French Quarter

"JELLY ROLL" MORTON HOME
1443 Frenchmen Street - 7th Ward

The home of "Jelly Roll" Morton on Frenchmen Street appears to be abandoned. There is no plaque signifying the importance of this jazz-related structure save a poignant framed photo of Morton sitting in the window.

"JELLY ROLL" MORTON LAMP
Robert E. Nims Jazz Walk of Fame - Algiers Point

SEVENTH WARD MUSICIANS

The Seventh Ward is opposite Esplanade Avenue from the Sixth Ward and, like those neighborhoods, was a predominantly Creole of Color residential area. The list of former residents from the Seventh Ward is impressive and includes Paul Barbarin, Barney Bigard, Lizzie Miles, "Jelly Roll" Morton, Manuel Perez, Buddy Petit, Omer Simeon and Lorenzo Tio Jr. Today, the Seventh Ward retains much of its historic appearance. NPS

Pianist, bandleader and composer, "Jelly Roll" Morton (1890-1940) lived at 1443 Frenchmen Street in the 7th Ward of New Orleans. He was probably born in Mississippi and his family moved here when he was very young. He began playing in bars and houses of prostitution when he was about ten years of age. He was also known at Ferdinand Joseph LaMenthe or LaMothe. His business card declared that he was the "originator of jazz."

MUNICIPAL AUDITORIUM

MUNICIPAL AUDITORIUM DETAIL
Morris F. X. Jeff Sr. Municipal Auditorium
Congo Square - Tremé

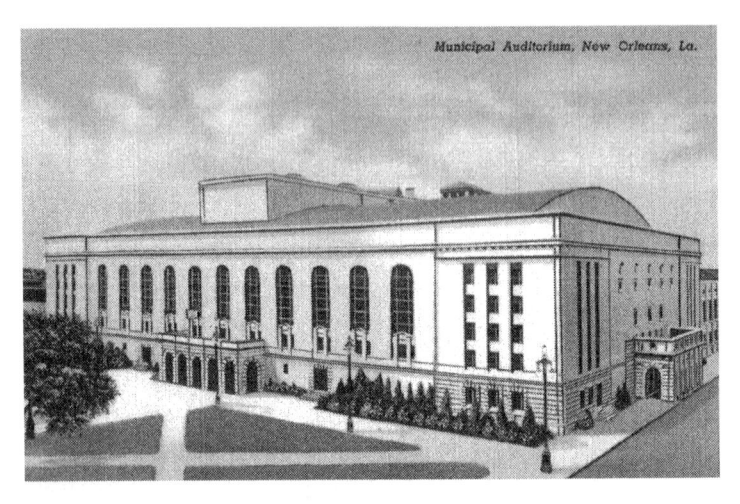

Designed in 1929 in the Italian Renaissance style by architects Favrot & Livaudais, the Municipal Auditorium is a large arena-style facility that can be divided into two separate theaters. Innumerable events with jazz have taken place here over the years including about half of Louis Armstrong's return-trip performances. NPS

NEW ORLEANS MUSICAL LEGENDS PARK
Edison Park - 311 Bourbon Street - French Quarter

This small park tucked away in the 300 block of Bourbon Street was developed in 2007 by the New Orleans Musical Legends Foundation. The park features life size statues of many New Orleans musicians such as Fats Domino, Pete Fountain, Louis Prima, Al Hirt, Ronnie Kole, Chris Owens, Irma Thomas and Allen Toussaint.

> **THE NEW ORLEANS MUSICIANS TOMB**
>
> This historic tomb which since the 19th century had interred the Sacred Union Society and the Barbarin Family now also acts as the New Orleans Musicians Tomb. The first burial was that of Lloyd Washington from the Ink Spots on October 23, 2004. The idea to provide free burial to musicians was conceived by Anna Ross Twichell. Burial space was donated by the Barbarin Family and the tomb was restored by Friends of New Orleans Cemeteries. The iron cross was forged and the blue note was cast by glass artist Mitchell Gaudet.

MUSICIANS' TOMB
Barbarin Family Tomb
St. Louis Cemetery #1
Basin and St Louis Streets - Tremé

There are actually two Barbarin family tombs in New Orleans cemeteries. This one in St. Louis Cemetery #1 is also known as the New Orleans Musicians' Tomb. It was originally used by the Sacred Union Society in the 19th Century. The Barbarin family has made this tomb available for all New Orleans musicians, rich and poor. The first such burial here was that of singer Lloyd Washington of the Ink Spots in 2004.

Jazz drummer Paul Barbarin's tomb can be found in St. Louis Cemetery #2, which is also the resting place for Danny Barker and his wife, Louisa "Blue Lu" Barker.

MUSICIAN'S UNION HALL
Exchange Alley - French Quarter

Over the years, the Musicians Mutual Protection Union, A. F. of M. Local 174, had several locations on this block, including 132, 134 and 116 Exchange. An early leadership struggle between bandleaders George De Droit and William Braun resulted in rival groups trying to occupy the same headquarters. NPS

MUSICIANS' VILLAGE
Ellis Marsalis Center for Music
Musicians' Village Park
1901 Bartholomew Street - Upper 9th Ward

Musicians' Village is a post-Katrina cultural initiative created to replace flood damaged housing in a section of the Upper Ninth Ward. The village covers an area bounded by North Roman, Alvar and North Johnson Streets, including a section of Bartholomew Street.

The centerpiece of Musicians' Village is The Ellis Marsalis Center for Music. The building houses 17,000 square feet of education and performance space and is a gathering place for the community. The goal of the Center is to channel the talents of the residents of Musicians' Village, providing a vital resource for sustaining the music culture of New Orleans.

ISIDORE NEWMAN MEMORIAL BANDSTAND
Audubon Park - Uptown

During the early 1920s, a regular series of band concerts were held here on Sundays during the summer months. There were also complimentary weekly concerts featuring the Jerusalem Temple Shrine Band, the New Orleans Police Band, the Sons of Shriners Band and the Jewish Children's Band. Isidore Newman was one of the earliest benefactors of Audubon Park.

NEW ORLEANS ATHLETIC CLUB
222 N. Rampart Street - French Quarter

The members of both Tom Brown's Band from Dixie and the Original Dixieland Jazz Band played here before heading north. The Boswell Sisters were discovered while singing here and immediately signed to a tour on the Orpheum Circuit. NPS

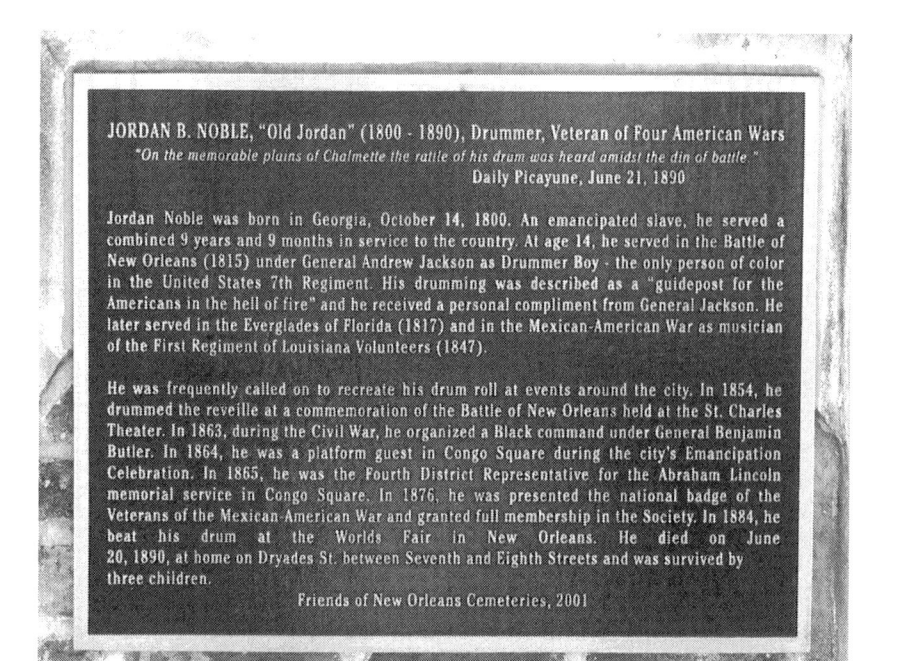

> **JORDAN B. NOBLE, "Old Jordan" (1800 - 1890), Drummer, Veteran of Four American Wars**
> *"On the memorable plains of Chalmette the rattle of his drum was heard amidst the din of battle."*
> Daily Picayune, June 21, 1890
>
> Jordan Noble was born in Georgia, October 14, 1800. An emancipated slave, he served a combined 9 years and 9 months in service to the country. At age 14, he served in the Battle of New Orleans (1815) under General Andrew Jackson as Drummer Boy - the only person of color in the United States 7th Regiment. His drumming was described as a "guidepost for the Americans in the hell of fire" and he received a personal compliment from General Jackson. He later served in the Everglades of Florida (1817) and in the Mexican-American War as musician of the First Regiment of Louisiana Volunteers (1847).
>
> He was frequently called on to recreate his drum roll at events around the city. In 1854, he drummed the reveille at a commemoration of the Battle of New Orleans held at the St. Charles Theater. In 1863, during the Civil War, he organized a Black command under General Benjamin Butler. In 1864, he was a platform guest in Congo Square during the city's Emancipation Celebration. In 1865, he was the Fourth District Representative for the Abraham Lincoln memorial service in Congo Square. In 1876, he was presented the national badge of the Veterans of the Mexican-American War and granted full membership in the Society. In 1884, he beat his drum at the Worlds Fair in New Orleans. He died on June 20, 1890, at home on Dryades St. between Seventh and Eighth Streets and was survived by three children.
>
> Friends of New Orleans Cemeteries, 2001

"OLD JORDAN" NOBLE TOMB
St. Louis Cemetery #2 - Square #3
N. Claiborne Avenue at Bienville Street - Tremé

Jordan B. Noble, a 14-year-old emancipated slave, was responsible for drumming the long roll at the Battle of New Orleans. He was the only African American to serve in the 7th Regiment under the command of General Andrew Jackson. Noble also served as principal musician during the Mexican War with the 1st Regiment, Louisiana Volunteers. He died in 1890, a veteran of four American wars. A drum owned by Noble is among other military artifacts on display at the Louisiana State Museum.

"... the rattle of his drum was heard amidst the din of battle."
- Daily Picayune, June 21, 1890

THE NO-NAME THEATER
1025 Canal Street - Central Business District

Here was another small movie theater that featured New Orleans musicians in its pit. The interesting name was the brainchild of Vic Perez, who opened the theater with a contest to name it. Perez, who was too cheap to award the cash prize, said none of the entries were acceptable and the theater would forever have no name. NPS

DAVE "BOB" OGDEN
2620 Milan Street - Uptown

Dave "Bob" Ogden (1914-1991) lived at 2620 Milan Street from 1961 to 1991. The son of drummer Dave Ogden, he studied at Xavier University and jammed with Earl Bostic. In 1937 he toured with Ida Cox in "The Darktown Scandals," played and recorded with Roy Brown's Mighty, Mighty Men, played in 1938-1941 with "Fats" Pinchon on the Steamer Capitol, and with Dave Bartholomew, "Papa" Celestin and briefly, Sidney Bechet. In 1947 he was in Earl M. Barnes's band. In the 1960s-70s he played mostly on Bourbon Street at the Paddock Lounge and also Maison Bourbon and Tradition Hall. PRC

OLD ABSINTHE HOUSE
240 Bourbon Street - French Quarter

Pianists who have played here include Steve Lewis, Frank Froeba, Burnell Santiago and Walter "Fats" Pichon. Louis Armstrong was the attraction here during his return trip to New Orleans in 1955. NPS

Robert E. Nims Jazz Walk of Fame - Algiers Point

JOSEPH "KING" OLIVER
2712 Dryades Street - Central City

Cornetist, bandleader and composer, Joseph "King" Oliver (1885-1938) lived at 2712 Dryades Street in 1916. Born in Abend, Louisiana, he started playing around 1904 with the Onward Brass Band, then the Allen Brass band, the Superior Orchestra, the Eagle Band, the Magnolia Orchestra, Richard M. Jones at Abadie's and as co-leader of the Ory-Oliver Band at Pete Lala's. He left for Chicago in 1918 achieving world renown with his Creole Band. Louis Armstrong joined the band in 1922 and their combined talents on recordings continue to delight and astound listeners. Oliver was an excellent accompanist, made superb recordings with "Jelly Roll" Morton and composed many jazz standards. PRC

ORPHEUM THEATRE

TERRACOTTA FAÇADE DETAIL
129 University Place - Central Business District

The Orpheum Circuit Company moved to this location in 1921. Conductor Emile Tosso's Orpheum Symphony Orchestra featured many jazz musicians including cornet player Johnny De Droit. The later house band also had jazz musicians including trumpeter Howard Reed, trombonist Jac Assunto and saxophonist Al Gallodoro. NPS

Robert E. Nims Jazz Walk of Fame - Algiers Point

EDWARD "KID" ORY
2135 Jackson Avenue - Central City

Trombonist, saxophonist, composer and bandleader, Edward "Kid" Ory (1886-1973) lived at 2135 Jackson Avenue in Central City from 1910 until 1916. He led the Woodlawn Band in LaPlace and his own band in New Orleans. He recorded in Los Angeles with his Sunshine Band in 1922 and in Chicago with Louis Armstrong's Hot Five, Joseph "King" Oliver and "Jelly Roll" Morton's Red Hot Peppers. His hit composition, "Muskrat Ramble," has gone through many reincarnations.   PRC

Music Street New Orleans

CHRIS OWENS
New Orleans Musical Legends Park - French Quarter

Hilton Walk of Fame - CBD

PABLO CASALS'S OBELISK
Besthoff Sculpture Garden - City Park
Armand Pierre Fernandez - 1983

PADDOCK LOUNGE
315 Bourbon Street

This nightspot with a horseracing theme was run by equestrian Steve Valenti and later by his wife. The band in the early 1950s was Oscar "Papa" Celestin's and then after his death, Octave Crosby's Band. The off-night group was Narvin Kimball's Gentlemen of Jazz. NPS

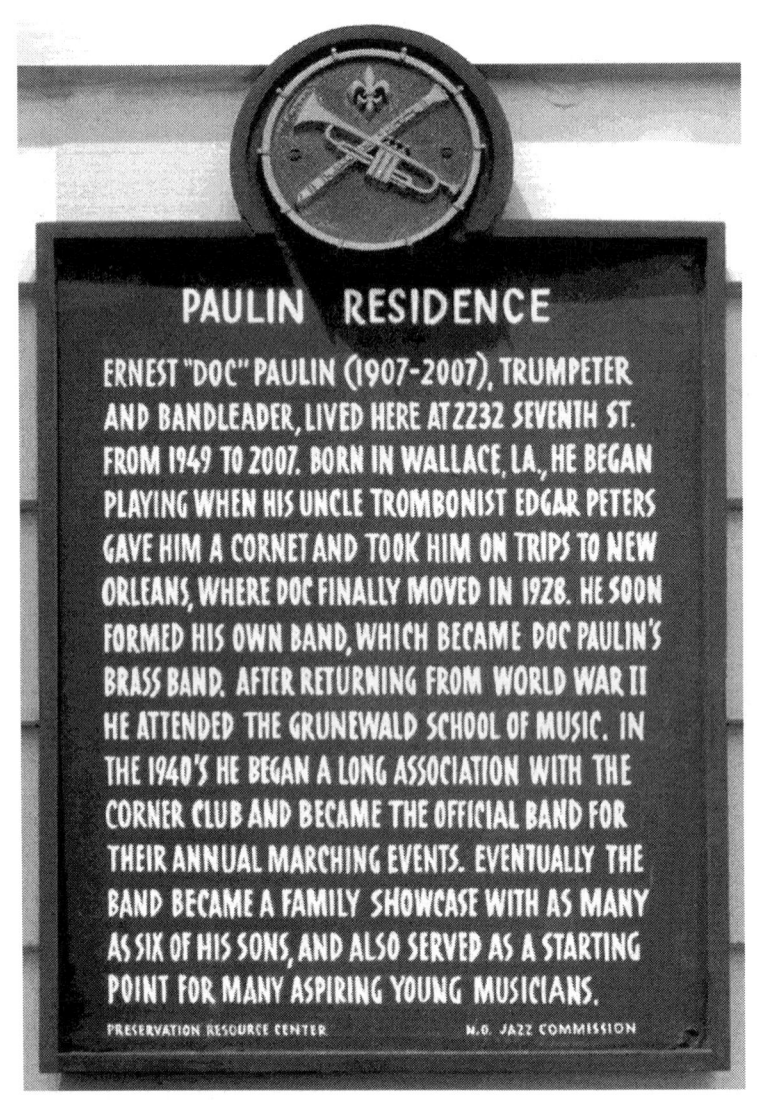

ERNEST "DOC" PAULIN
2232 Seventh Street - Central City

THE PICKWICK CLUB
1030 Canal Street - Central Business District

This club's design was based on a Venetian Palazzo prototype in 1896. It had a Turkish lounge and a roof garden. Its three-term president, music store impresario Philip Werlein III, undoubtedly made sure that the latest in New Orleans music was played on the premises. The building has now been heavily modified. NPS

ALPHONSE FLORISTAN PICOU
1601 Ursulines Ave - Tremé

Clarinetist, composer and bandleader, Alphonse Picou (1879-1961) lived at 1601 Ursulines Avenue from 1960 to 1961. He was famous as an early pioneer of jazz, for his transposition of the "High Society" piccolo solo for clarinet as a member of the early Tuxedo Brass Band and the later "Papa" Celestin Band. He played at the Paddock Lounge on Bourbon Street in the 1940s and 50s serving occasionally as the bandleader. PRC

PIER 600
600 Bourbon Street - French Quarter

Starting as Dan's International Settlement Club in the 1950s and ending as Dan's Bateau Lounge in the 1960s, this location was also Dan's Pier 600 in between. Proprietor Dan Levy showcased Jack Bachman, Lester Bouchon and Len Ferguson at the first, and Pete Fountain, Al Hirt, Bob Havens and Godfrey Hirsch, at the second.

ARMAND JOHN PIRON
1818 Columbus Street - 7th Ward

Violinist, composer, publisher and orchestra leader, Armand John Piron (1888-1943) lived at 1818 Columbus Street from 1912 to 1915. He ran the Williams & Piron Publishing Company with Clarence Williams and published many of his own compositions. His Piron Orchestra with Peter Bocage, Steve Lewis, Lorenzo Tio Jr. and others, was a "society band" that played in New Orleans at Spanish Fort, the Southern Yacht Club, the New Orleans Country Club and the St. Charles Hotel. PRC

THE PLAZA THEATER
841 Canal Street

The Plaza featured movies and local music. Mary Nadal, later the wife of Robert Hoffman, accompanied silent pictures here with a piano equipped with an "Orgatron" device that converted its sound to an organ. NPS

LA POÉTESSE
Besthoff Sculpture Garden - City Park
Ossip Zadkine - 1953

THE POPEYE BEER PARLOR
1135 Decatur Street - French Quarter

The Popeye was one of the 1930s Decatur Street establishments that managed to last for almost a decade. Musicians who played here included Billie & Dee Dee Pierce, Wilbert Tillman, George Lewis, Harold Dejan, Ernie Cagnolatti, Kid Howard, Lionel Ferbos and John Brunious. NPS

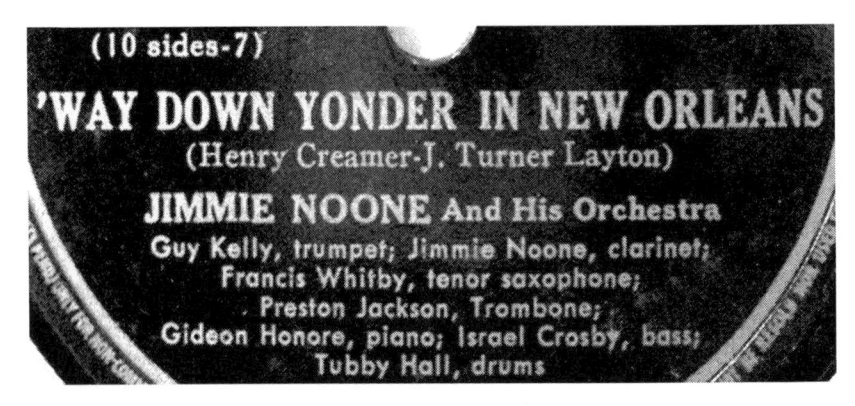

(10 sides-7)
'WAY DOWN YONDER IN NEW ORLEANS
(Henry Creamer-J. Turner Layton)
JIMMIE NOONE And His Orchestra
Guy Kelly, trumpet; Jimmie Noone, clarinet;
Francis Whitby, tenor saxophone;
Preston Jackson, Trombone;
Gideon Honore, piano; Israel Crosby, bass;
Tubby Hall, drums

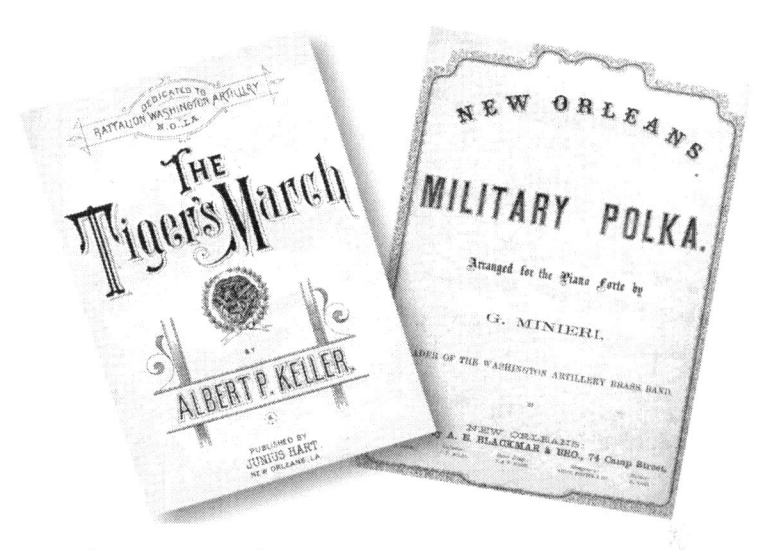

Popp Bandstand was dedicated on July 4, 1917 as a gift to City Park from millionaire John F. Popp. The beautiful rotunda was designed by Emile Weil. The popular outdoor concerts held here took on military and patriotic themes due to the proximity of the Great War and lasted well into the era of World War II. Concerts were given by the Louisiana Infantry Military Band as well as J. K. Snee's Regimental Band. For many years the American Federation of Musicians provided orchestras for regular concerts.

POPP BANDSTAND
Dreyfous Drive - City Park

All Steel Steamer "PRESIDENT" On the Mississippi

THE PRESIDENT

Early jazz also developed aboard steamboats sailing out of the city. On the Mississippi River, the S.S. Capitol, Sidney and the President were among the best-known riverboats to feature jazz. The S.S. Mandeville and the Susquehanna used jazz to entertain passengers on excursions on Lake Pontchartrain. None of the vessels associated with early jazz still exist. NPS

Robert E. Nims Jazz Walk of Fame - Algiers Point

LOUIS PRIMA
New Orleans Musical Legends Park
311 Bourbon Street - French Quarter
Stephen Gibson - Sculptor

THE ANGEL GABRIEL
Louis Prima Tomb
Metairie Cemetery - Section 88 - Lakewood
Alexei Kazantsey - Sculptor

Jazz, Rock and Rhythm & Blues

PROFESSOR LONGHAIR

PROFESSOR LONGHAIR
Tipitina's Walk Of Fame
501 Napoleon Avenue - East Riverside

PROFESSOR LONGHAIR MURAL
Oretha Castle Haley Boulevard - Central City
Mayor's Office of Economic Development

PROFESSOR LONGHAIR SQUARE
501 Napoleon Avenue Neutral Ground - East Riverside

PYTHIAN TEMPLE
234 Loyola Avenue - Central Business District

The imposing Pythian Temple Building represents an economic achievement for people of color in the city. It had a fashionable roof garden, the Pythian Roof, which was later enclosed to form the Parisian Garden Room. Cornetist Manuel Perez played regularly in this room and it was later managed by composer, bandleader and publisher A. J. Piron. NPS

FLORENCIO RAMOS
4505 Dryades Street - Uptown

Music Street New Orleans

RILEY RESIDENCE

TEDDY RILEY (1924-1992), TRUMPET PLAYER AND BANDLEADER, LIVED HERE AT 914 VALENCE STREET FROM 1962 TO 1992. HE PLAYED WITH JOE AVERY'S BAND, JEANETTE KIMBALL, THE MUSIC MASTERS, DON RAYMOND, THE HERBERT LEARY ORCH., THE DOOKY CHASE ORCH., SIDNEY DESVIGNE, ROY BROWN AND THE MIGHTY MIGHTY MEN, EARL BOSTIC, FATS DOMINO, LOUIS COTTRELL, AND THE KID JOHNSON ORCH. HE ALSO PLAYED WITH HENRY ALLEN'S BRASS BAND, HAROLD DEJAN'S OLYMPIA BRASS BAND, GEORGE WILLIAMS' BRASS BAND, AND HIS OWN ROYAL BRASS BAND. HE WAS CHOSEN TO PLAY TAPS ON LOUIS ARMSTRONG'S "WAIF'S HOME" CORNET AT THE LOUIS ARMSTRONG MEMORIAL SERVICE IN NEW ORLEANS IN 1971.

N.O. JAZZ COMMISSION PRESERVATION RESOURCE CENTER

TEDDY RILEY
914 Valence Street - West Riverside

MASTER SERIES: 240-A
VOCAL CHARLES BROWN
"NEW ORLEANS BLUES"
(Leon René)
JOHNNY MOORE'S THREE BLAZERS
Charles Brown, Piano
Johnny Moore, Guitar
Eddie Williams, Bass

JOHN P. ROBICHAUX
4727 Camp Street - Uptown

Violinist, drummer, accordionist, bandleader and teacher, John P. Robichaux (1867-1938) lived at 4727 Camp Street from 1909 until 1927. He played with the Excelsior Brass Band, then formed his own Robichaux Orchestra, a successful "society" orchestra which had engagements at Lincoln Park, Antoine's Restaurant, the Grunewald Hotel, St. Catherine's Hall and La Louisiane Restaurant. His group was also the house orchestra at the Lyric Theater from 1919 until 1927. He continued teaching students for another decade. PRC

ROMA'S CAFÉ
1003 Decatur St. - French Quarter

This cafe on the second floor above Roma's Restaurant featured various bands during the 1930s, including clarinetist Luke Schiro. His drummer was Joe Stephens, son of Jack Laine's legendary drummer, "Ragbaby" Stephens.

ROOSEVELT HOTEL
"The Blue Room"
123 Baronne Street - CBD

Built in 1908, the Grunewald Hotel later became the Roosevelt Hotel. A major music policy has prevailed since its inception. The Grunewald Cave showcased Johnny De Droit's Band dressed as elves. The Roosevelt's Blue Room had major musical acts such as Ted Lewis, the Mills Brothers, Sophie Tucker and Bob Crosby's Band. The WWL radio studios, home of the long-running Dawnbusters and New Orleans Jazz Club programs, were also here. NPS

ROOTS OF MUSIC CULTURAL GARDEN

MITCHELL J. LANDRIEU
MAYOR

CITY COUNCIL MEMBERS

JACQUELYN BRECHTEL CLARKSON	AT-LARGE
ERIC GRANDERSON	AT-LARGE
SUSAN G. GUIDRY	DISTRICT A
STACY HEAD	DISTRICT B
KRISTIN GISLESON PALMER	DISTRICT C
CYNTHIA HEDGE-MORRELL	DISTRICT D
JON D. JOHNSON	DISTRICT E

HAMILTON ANDERSON ASSOCIATES
LANDSCAPE ARCHITECT

A.M.E. DISASTER RECOVERY SERVICES, INC.
GENERAL CONTRACTOR

SCULPTURES WERE GENEROUSLY FUNDED BY THE EDWARD WISNER DONATION
2011

ROOTS OF MUSIC CULTURAL GARDEN
Louis Armstrong Park
North Rampart Street at St. Ann - Tremé

KERMIT RUFFINS MURAL
Daniel Fuselier - Artist
1500 N. Claiborne Avenue - Tremé

SAENGER THEATER

SAENGER THEATER DETAIL
1111 Canal Street - Central Business District
North Rampart Street Façade

The Saenger was designed as an atmospheric theater (with stars and clouds) by architect Emile Weil and opened in 1927. It still has its Robert-Morton organ and a rising orchestra pit for fifty musicians. Included in its various musical groups were trumpeters Johnny De Droit, Mike Caplan and Louis Prima, banjoist, Steve Loyacano and clarinetist, Tony Parenti. Castro Carazo, who led the orchestra, later collaborated with Governor Huey P. Long on several compositions. NPS

SATCHMO SUMMERFEST
Old U.S. Mint - French Quarter

On the first weekend of August, we celebrate the life of Louis Armstrong with a glorious weekend of music and food. You can hear traditional and contemporary jazz as well as the city's best brass bands. Special events include Red Bean Alley with local cuisine, second line parades, a jazz mass at the historic St. Augustine Church and a red beans and rice luncheon.

SEA-SAINT STUDIO SITE
3809 Clematis Street - Edgewood Park/Gentilly

During the 1975 Carnival season, Paul and Linda McCartney recorded the Wings' album, *Venus and Mars*, at this Gentilly recording studio owned by Allen Toussaint and Marshall Sehorn. They also produced several singles here including, "My Carnival." They generally completed a session in the wee hours of the morning where they would always encounter groups of fans in the parking lot waiting for autographs. We were often successful.

SECOND LINE

NEW ORLEANS MARCHING BRASS BAND
Louis Armstrong Park
N. Rampart and St. Ann Streets - Tremé
Sheleen Jones-Adenle - 2010

    Traditionally, a second line is a spontaneous parade created by followers that develops around a main or "first line" of a Carnival parade, marching band or a jazz funeral. A second line might also form around the Mardi Gras Indians as they walk the streets of Tremé. The second liners dance along the route traditionally carrying umbrellas and waving handkerchiefs. The term can also be used as a verb. Audience members at Jazz Fest performances often second line through the crowd.

    The late artist, John Scott, wrote that the early Africans in Congo Square performed their sacred circle dance which evolved into the Bamboula and eventually what we know today as a second line.

"In New Orleans, we're born with music.
We live with music. They bury you with music."
- John Scott

NEW ORLEANS MARCHING BRASS BAND

JUST BEFORE 1900, LOCAL BLACK MARCHING BANDS BEGAN TO IMPROVISE ON RAGS, HYMNS, BLUES, AND EUROPEAN MARCHES IN A NEW STYLE, LATER CALLED "JAZZ." OFTEN THE TRAINING GROUND FOR JAZZ GREATS, BRASS BANDS REMAIN A POPULAR FIXTURE IN SOCIAL CLUB PARADES AND JAZZ FUNERALS. THEIR EXCITING MUSIC IS OFTEN ACCOMPANIED BY A DANCE CALLED "THE SECOND LINE."

SCULPTOR: SHELEEN JONES-ADENLE
DEDICATED APRIL, 2010
THIS SCULPTURE WAS GENEROUSLY FUNDED BY
THE EDWARD WISNER DONATION

SCHILLING RESIDENCE

GEORGE "HAPPY" SCHILLING (1886-1964) TROMBONIST, GUITARIST, AND BANDLEADER, LIVED HERE AT 3249 ANNUNCIATION STREET FROM 1914 UNTIL 1915. HE PLAYED GUITAR IN GERBRECHT'S STRING BAND, THEN TROMBONE IN JACK LAINE'S RELIANCE BRASS BANDS AND JOHNNY FISHER'S BRASS BAND, LED SCHILLING'S "BLACK AND WHITE" BRASS BAND, AND PLAYED STRING BASS IN GEORGE PAOLETTI'S CONCERT BAND. SCHILLING'S DIXIE JAZZ BAND HAD A CONSTANT, DIZZYING ARRAY OF SPOT JOBS FOR GROUPS INCLUDING THE AMERICAN LEGION, THE POLICE PICNIC, THE RETAIL GROCER'S ASSN., THE STREETCARMEN'S ASSN., VOLUNTEER FIRE COMPANIES, AND WARD MEETINGS. HE PLAYED FOR CARNIVAL BALLS, FUNERALS, HORSE RACES, AND HAD A STEADY JOB AT HEINEMAN PARK OR PELICAN STADIUM, PLAYING FOR NEW ORLEANS PELICANS BASEBALL GAMES.

N.O. JAZZ COMMISSION   PRESERVATION RESOURCE CENTER

GEORGE "HAPPY" SCHILLING
3249 Annunciation Street - Uptown
822 Harmony Street - Irish Channel
1020 Pleasant Street - Irish Channel
818 Toledano - Irish Channel

PAUL SAREBRESOLE
1359 St. Anthony Street - New Marigny

Composer and performer, Paul Sarebresole (1871-1911) lived at 1359 St. Anthony Street in 1911. In 1897, he composed New Orleans first rag "Roustabout Rag," an innovative piece and one of several other pieces he composed both the notable "Come Clean" and "Get Your Habit's On," each containing abundant illustrations of New Orleans urban folk culture. PRC

SPANISH FORT

Spanish Fort, the Coney Island of New Orleans, La.

Spanish Fort carried the entertainment a step further than West End. The amusement park included several restaurants, a beer garden, casinos, and even a couple of cabarets. As jazz began to develop as a music form, musicians playing at the restaurants and cabarets at Spanish Fort naturally began to pick it up. The area become one of the hottest spots for hearing the jazz of Armand J. Piron's New Orleans Orchestra as well as "Papa" Celestin's Band.

The Lake Pontchartrain shore includes Bucktown, West End, Spanish Fort, Milneburg and Little Woods. Historically, the lakefront was a resort area where brass bands played at amusement parks, dance pavilions, saloons, picnics, and family "camps." Early jazz musicians of all races and economic classes performed in groups at the lakefront, which was important as a place where musical ideas and techniques were shared and mixed. Joseph "Sharkey" Bonano was born in Milneburg. Most of the lakefront relating to jazz history was irreversibly altered in the late 1920s when the shoreline from West End to the east of Milneburg was extended about 2,000 feet into Lake Pontchartrain. Important sites that were obliterated by the reclamation project and other efforts included Tranchina's and the Tokyo Gardens at Spanish Fort, the boardwalk and stilt camps at Milneburg as well as the West End Roof Garden. Only a few isolated and altered structures related to early jazz remain today. NPS

SPARICIO'S SALOON
1136 Decatur Street - French Quarter

Johnny Sparicio was an early New Orleans violinist, music instructor and bartender, and later a Milneburg dairy farmer, who was associated with bandleader Jack Laine and clarinetist Alcide "Yellow" Nunez. This was one of four bars operated by the Sparicios, and most likely the hangout for Laine and his musicians. NPS

STEPHENS RESIDENCE

PHILIP HORACE "DIDDIE" STEPHENS (1888-1944), DRUMMER, LIVED HERE AT 931 MANDEVILLE STREET IN 1921. ONE OF FOUR DRUMMERS IN THE VERY MUSICAL STEPHENS FAMILY, HE WAS A LONG-TIME MEMBER OF JACK LAINE'S RELIANCE BRASS BAND. HE ALSO PLAYED WITH HAPPY SCHILLING'S DIXIE JAZZ BAND, SCHILLING'S BRASS BAND, ERNEST GIARDINA'S BAND, AND EDDIE EDWARDS' BAND.

2002 N.O. JAZZ COMMISSION • PRESERVATION RESOURCE CENTER

PHILIP HORACE "DIDDIE" STEPHENS
931 Mandeville Street - Marigny

Stephens also lived at 2563 N. Roman Street from 1923 until 1944.

> **STORYVILLE**
> Created 1897 and closed 1917, New Orleans' famous legalized red-light district was in this area. Among many great jazz musicians on the scene here were "King" Oliver, "Jelly Roll" Morton, Louis Armstrong, Tony Jackson, and Jimmie Noone.

STORYVILLE

Not much is left of Storyville except its reputation, and the music. Storyville was a legal red light district that existed from 1897-1917. If New Orleans is the birthplace of jazz, Storyville is the mother. The Krauss Condominium complex now occupies the 200 block of Basin Street where the majority of the infamous sporting houses once stood. One of three remaining Storyville buildings is Frank Early's Saloon at Bienville and Crozat Streets. Tony Jackson lived upstairs where he probably composed "Pretty Baby." Jackson was the only piano player who "Jelly Roll" Morton admitted was better than he was.

The other two remaining establishments include Lulu White's Saloon and Joe Victor's Saloon.

Jackson, "Jelly Roll" and Joe "King" Oliver were among the most celebrated musicians known to play the bordellos of the "District." Almost every early jazz musician got their start in Storyville.

In order to help his family pay the bills, a very young Louis Armstrong hauled coal into the brothels and dance halls where he was constantly exposed to this exciting new sound, among other things.

> 402154
> SPEED 78
> R. 531
> NEW RHYTHM STYLE SERIES, No. 14
> **BASIN STREET BLUES**
> (Williams)
> LOUIS ARMSTRONG AND HIS ORCHESTRA

STORYVILLE POSTCARD
"Down the Line"
200 Block of Basin Street - Tremé

Storyville, also known as the "District," was the legendary tenderloin of New Orleans which operated legally between 1897 and 1917. Prostitution was the primary business in Storyville, but music and entertainment were prominent sidelines. While jazz was not born in Storyville, as legend has it, the district helped expose the new music to a wider audience. Several brothels had a piano "professor," but most jazz musicians in the district were employed in dance bands, clubs and restaurants such as Pete Lala's, the 101 Ranch, the Fewclothes Cabaret, the Tuxedo Dance Hall and the Big 25. Virtually all Storyville structures were removed for the Iberville public housing project in the 1940s, and only three original structures and remnants remain. One of them, Frank Early's Saloon directly relates to the development of jazz. NPS

NORMA WALLACE'S HOUSE
1026 Conti Street - Tango Belt - French Quarter

This brick structure was the site of the last operating bordello in the Tango Belt. The "Belt" was the corner of the Vieux Carre bounded by Iberville, Dauphine, St. Louis and Rampart Streets. Once an area of respectable theaters and cabarets, it quickly supported the milder side of the sporting life, prize fighting, proto-jazz music, alcohol and dance halls. When Storyville's future became uncertain, drugs and prostitution completed the picture here. NPS

TANGO BELT

The Tango Belt was in the French Quarter just across Basin and North Rampart Streets from Storyville, and there was a symbiotic relationship between the two entertainment areas. The Tango Belt had numerous saloons, cabarets, nightclubs, and three large theaters that employed jazz musicians, including the Oasis Cabaret, the Elite, Butzie Fernandez, the Haymarket and Ringside Cafés and the Black Orchid. The name Tango Belt derived from a 1915 newspaper article that used that name to describe this district. At its peak, the area had one of the highest concentrations of commercial jazz venues in the city. NPS

TERPSICHORE

BIRTH OF A MUSE
Terpsichore at Prytania Street - Garden District
Kim Bernadas - 2011

It is the mission of all artists to awaken the magic and wonder within us all. The muses, according to Greek mythology, are goddesses who inspire the creation of the arts. They whisper in the ear, light the fire within and stimulate the creative process of every artist. Expressed here is Terpsichore, emerging from a trumpet flower, to begin her life in celebration of music, song and dance. Plaque Inscription

"She remains one of America's most distinctive and classic singers, a treasure from the golden age of soul music who remains as compelling and powerful as ever ..." -Rounder Records

IRMA THOMAS
New Orleans Musical Legends Park
311 Bourbon Street - French Quarter
Stephen Gibson - Sculptor

Blues, R&B, soul and gospel, the "Soul Queen of New Orleans" does it all. She first auditioned for a record company when she was 13 years old. Irma remains an annual fixture at Jazz Fest and continues her popular Mother's Day appearances at the Audubon Zoo.

ALLEN TOUSSAINT

Mother-In-Law Lounge Mural
1500 N. Claiborne Avenue - Tremé
Daniel Fuselier - Artist

New Orleans Musical Legends Park
311 Bourbon Street - French Quarter
Stephen Gibson - Sculptor

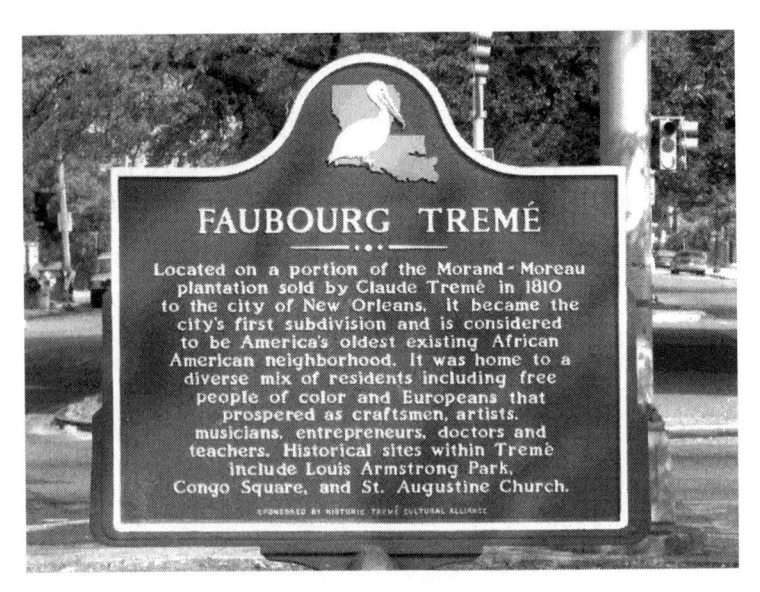

FAUBOURG TREMÉ HISTORICAL MARKER
North Claiborne Avenue at Esplanade - Tremé
Historic Tremé Cultural Alliance

Tremé started as an early French-speaking Creole of Color community and later became a culturally mixed neighborhood typical of New Orleans. The residents of Tremé take great pride in their history and musical traditions. Many downtown marching clubs parade through the streets; in fact the area has one of the highest concentrations of jazz parading in the city. The neighborhood includes Armstrong Park and Congo Square. Historically, the Tremé neighborhood was home to several early musicians including George Lewis, Chris Kelly, Jimmie Noone and Henry Ragas. It had a number of important social halls and commercial venues. Today much of Tremé looks as it did at the turn of the century when jazz was evolving. Nonetheless, demolitions for a cultural center (later incorporated into Armstrong Park) and other urban renewal projects removed several important jazz sites including Economy Hall and the Gypsy Tea Room. Equity Hall, later known as Jeune Amis Hall, remains.

Contiguous with Tremé, the Sixth Ward neighborhood on the lake side of Claiborne Avenue is a residential area that was home to Sidney and Leonard Bechet, Freddie and Louis Keppard, Alphonse Picou, Kid Rena and other predominantly Creole of Color jazz musicians. Claiborne Avenue, which divides Tremé from the rest of the Sixth Ward, was formerly a tree-lined promenade that was frequently used for marching club parades, Mardi Gras and other community activities. However, construction of the Interstate 10 viaduct down Claiborne in the 1960s dramatically altered the community landscape. In spite of the intrusion of the interstate and poor economic conditions, social aid and pleasure clubs and mutual aid societies continue the jazz parade tradition in the Sixth Ward. NPS

Jazz, Rock and Rhythm & Blues

TREMÉ UNDER THE BRIDGE
N. Claiborne Avenue - Tremé
Between St. Bernard and Orleans Avenues

The bridge support columns are now decorated with beautiful paintings by local artists representing famous African Americans and important events in the civil rights, culture and music history of New Orleans. Today, "Tremé under the Bridge" is the location for Mardi Gras Indian gatherings, jazz funerals, brass bands and a monthly neighborhood market.

TREMÉ NEIGHBORHOOD BANNER
Louis Armstrong Park - Tremé

THE TRIANON THEATER
814 Canal Street - Central Business District

This was a medium-sized house again featuring movies and music. Pianists such as Irwin Leclere possibly played here from 1918 into the 1920s. NPS

TUBA FATS SQUARE
St. Philip and N. Robertson - Tremé

This small park is dedicated to Anthony Lacen, otherwise known as Tuba Fats. He was a regular performer in Jackson Square and played with the Tuxedo, Olympia and Chosen Few Brass Bands. He passed away on January 11, 2004, at the age of 53. A free music festival is held here in Tremé just after Jazz Fest called, Tuba Fats Tuesday. It is sponsored by a neighborhood collective known as Sixth Ward International. The park is just down the block from The Candlelight Bar.

"KID" THOMAS VALENTINE
825 Vallette Street - Algiers Point

Trumpeter and bandleader, "Kid" Thomas Valentine (1897-1987) lived at 825 Vallette Street in 1928. Born in Reserve, Louisiana, he moved to Algiers in 1923. He played at Speck's Moulin Rouge in Marrero and Fireman's Hall in Westwego in the 1930s and formed the Algiers Stompers in the 1940s. He was among the first to play at the 1950s jam sessions that were the forerunner of Preservation Hall and then at the Hall starting in the 1960s. He toured Japan with clarinetist George Lewis and traveled throughout the world. PRC

JOE VICTOR'S SALOON
St. Louis and North Villere Streets - Storyville - Tremé

Joe Victor's Saloon is one of only three remaining buildings associated with Storyville.

VOODOO MUSIC-ARTS EXPERIENCE
City Park - 2013

BOOKER T. WASHINGTON AUDITORIUM
1201 South Roman Street - Central City

In 2013, Booker T. Washington High School succumbed to selective demolition due to Hurricane Katrina damage. It is being replaced with a new charter school. The historic auditorium, however, is being restored.

The auditorium was used for cultural and social events for African Americans such as choir recitals and labor rallies. An annual concert series presented by the Crescent Concerts Company featured Paul Robeson in 1942 and Marian Anderson in 1943. The year 1949 brought Louis Armstrong, Dizzy Gillespie and Mahalia Jackson to the Booker T stage.

WERLEIN'S FOR MUSIC
(The Palace Café)
605 Canal Street - Central Business District

Located in this building for over 75 years, Werlein's was one of New Orleans' leading music houses. Werlein's published music and sold instruments and supplies. Jazz bands often played outside the store on sidewalks and from bandwagons.

The central business district contained theaters, music companies and publishing houses that were part of a mainstream entertainment district in the early 20th century. Theaters featuring minstrel shows, ragtime, vaudeville and eventually jazz, included the Crescent, Lyric, Strand, No Name, Alamo, Plaza and Trianon. Publishers included Piron-Williams Publishing, Hackenjos Music Company, Junius Hart Piano House, L. Grunewald and Company and others who documented the floating folk strains and popular rags that contributed to early jazz. These businesses reflected how early jazz was affected by popular music and how that process was eventually reversed when jazz received national acclaim. NPS

WERLEIN'S MUSIC
333 Baronne Street - Central Business District

This was Werlein's first long-term location after the Civil War (1867-1877) and closely adjacent to their later Werlein Hall (1881-87) on the site of the current Le Pavillon Hotel. Werlein's has published music for 150 years and is one of the oldest family owned retail music businesses in the United States. NPS

WEST END

Joseph "King" Oliver wrote the very popular jazz tune, "West End Blues" as a tribute to West End Summer and Winter Resort which was located on the shore of Lake Pontchartrain at the mouth of New Basin Canal. West End was a very popular music, food, lodging and entertainment destination during the early days of jazz in New Orleans. The reputation of the resort was further enhanced by Louis Armstrong's popular recording of "West End Blues" in the 1920s.

WSMB RADIO
Maison Blanche Building
921 Canal Street - Central Business District

WSMB's studio was on the top floor of the Maison Blanche building for several decades. The postcard illustration depicts the large antennas that once rose from the roof of the building. The station was a joint venture of the Saenger Amusement Company and the Maison Blanche Department Store. The station had a long-time preference for jazz, initially as live music and later as recorded music. NPS

LULU WHITE'S SALOON
Basin Street at Bienville - Storyville - Tremé

Lulu White's Saloon is one of only three remaining buildings associated with Storyville. There was a second story which was destroyed during Hurricane Betsy. The famous guide to Storyville, the Blue Book, was published here. Emile "Stalebread" Lacoume and his "spasm" band most likely played on this very corner.

Just to the left of the saloon was Lulu White's four-story Mahogany Hall. The Octoroon Queen's adopted nephew, Spencer Williams, wrote the "Mahogany Hall Stomp" immortalizing the famous marble mansion. The song was eventually recorded by Louis Armstrong.

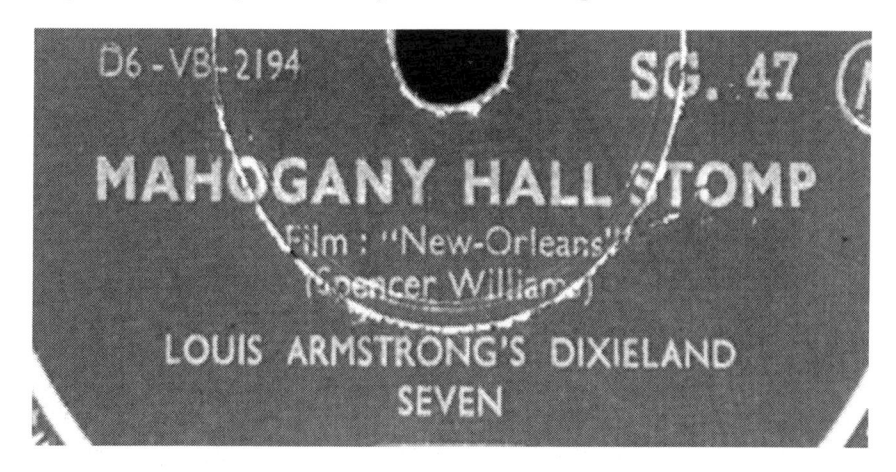

TOM ZIMMERMANN
4607 Freret Street - Uptown

Pianist and composer, Thomas C. "Tom" Zimmermann (1888-1923) lived at 4607 Freret Street from 1913 until 1915. He played piano in Jack Laine's Band, Johnny De Droit's Band, at the Tudor Theater and at Tom Anderson's Café in the Tango Belt. He composed "Buy A Bale," "Steamboat Days" and "Down at the Codfish Ball." PRC

PHILIP "PHIL" ZITO
1519 Camp Street - Uptown

Drummer and bandleader, Philip "Phil" Zito (1913-1998) lived at 1519 Camp Street from 1986 until 1991. He played in the Navy Band, at the Parisian Room with his own New Orleans International City Dixielanders, at the Club Morocco, at receptions for Presidents Eisenhower and Johnson and at many jazz concerts, dances, French Quarter clubs and Canal Street hotels. He led his own Big Band at the Treasure Chest Casino. He was also a long-time board member of Musicians' Union Local no. 174-496. PRC

"What we play is life."
- **Louis Armstrong**

Jazz, Rock and Rhythm & Blues

ABOUT THE AUTHOR

Kevin J. Bozant was born in the Upper 9th Ward of New Orleans – as luck would have it – just a few blocks from Huerstel's Bar and Little Pete's Seafood Restaurant. He is a local author, photographer and digital graphic designer for his publishing company, Po-Boy Press – New Orleans.

His professional experience includes Warner Brothers, CW and ABC television affiliates. Kevin specialized in sales, marketing, promotional graphics and special events coordination. He eventually became senior graphic designer for the news, sports and weather departments. He was font operator for fifteen seasons of *Friday Night Football* as well as *Saints Sideline* with Ed Daniels. Kevin provided technical assistance on location shoots for *Real New Orleans* with Ronnie Virgets, *Crescent City Country* with Kim Carson, co-produced *New Orleans after Midnight* with Bernie Cyrus and developed and co-produced *The Southern Garden* for Vitascope Television. He also served as studio graphics manager and question writer for Brandon Tartikoff's popular New Orleans trivia game show *N.O. It Alls*.

Kevin showcased his warped opinion of local politics and culture as writer and editor of the "Crescent City Crier" a political cartoon published by Gambit Weekly. He is author and editor of *Port & Burgundy 1840-1990: A Pictorial History* covering 150 years of St. Paul German Lutheran Church and Faubourg Marigny; *Quaint Essential New Orleans: A Crescent City Lexicon*; *African American New Orleans: a Guide to 100 Civil Rights, Culture and Jazz Sites*; *Crescent City Soldiers: Military Monuments of New Orleans* as well as *Music Street New Orleans: A Guide to 200 Jazz, Rock and Rhythm & Blues Sites*.

Kevin's favorite cultural experience was serving as personal assistant to Dr. Momus Alexander Morgus for his Halloween appearances at the Audubon Zoo.

poboypress@yahoo.com
www.amazon.com/author/kevinjbozant

Printed in Great Britain
by Amazon